THE AMATEUR

WIND INSTRUMENT

MAKER

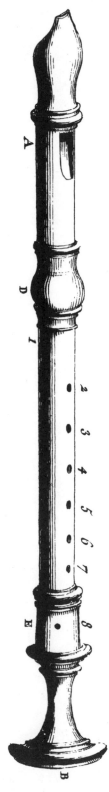

THE AMATEUR
WIND INSTRUMENT
MAKER

TREVOR ROBINSON

The University of Massachusetts Press 1973

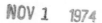

Contents

Illustrations

Tables

Preface

The making of musical instruments of any kind is a rewarding hobby because of the versatile craftsmanship that it calls for, and because the finished product continues to bring joy to the player long after it is made. In a society which enjoys an increasing amount of leisure it is essential that satisfying avocations be available, and I have decided to write this book to call attention to one of the most satisfying and one of the least exploited that I know. It is surprising that while amateur makers of violins, guitars, and harpsichords are a well-recognized group catered to by publishers and dealers in wood and supplies, amateur makers of wind instruments are almost nonexistent.

I have found instrument making to be a very rewarding hobby for the friendships it has initiated and cemented. Others who take it up will discover that they will find kindred spirits all over the world who will give freely of their knowledge and support. A few of these whom I wish to give special thanks for helping me with particular problems or for their general interest and encouragement are Friedrich von Huene; Mr. and Mrs. R. K. Lee, Jr.; Charles J. Lehrer; Kenneth C. Parker; and Narcissa Williamson.

There is no end to the process of learning better ways to make things. By the time this book appears, I should expect to have improved on some of my procedures; and after it has appeared, I shall look forward to receiving suggestions and corrections from my readers.

THE AMATEUR
WIND INSTRUMENT
MAKER

I
Introduction

The craftsman who embarks on the making of musical instruments must already have acquired some basic skills in woodworking and metalworking and must have a shop which is well equipped with common hand and power tools. It is perhaps superfluous to point out that he should also have an ear for music, because the finest appearing instrument is worthless if it can't be played and is nearly worthless if it is not pitched to agree with accepted standards. In this chapter I shall deal with some of the most general aspects of instrument making, and throughout the rest of the book I shall treat more specialized techniques and particular instruments.

Much can be done by trial and error and by copying successful instruments, but anyone who concerns himself for very long with musical instruments will probably want to learn more about the physics of sound production and the science of acoustics. For a good start in this direction I should like to refer him to the brief and clear book, *Horns, Strings, and Harmony*, by A. H. Benade.

Equipping the Shop

There are very few hand tools required in instrument making that will not be found in the average shop. A collection of tapered reamers is handy for enlarging tone holes and making the back bore on mouthpieces for brass instruments. Calipers are essential for measuring both inside and outside diameters.

Beyond the circular saw and drill press, which are probably stock items in the average shop, the major power tool for the instrument maker is a wood-turning lathe. Thirty inches between centers will permit making practically any instrument. A heavily constructed wood-turning lathe also serves for the metal spinning required to make brass instruments. A metalworking lathe is required to make special reamers for flutes and the larger recorders. It is useful for making brass mouthpieces, but these can be made on the woodworking lathe. A miniature lathe like the Unimat can be used for making brass mouthpieces and is also handy for turning small ivory rings. It is just possible to manage all of the turning operations for a soprano recorder on the Unimat. Basic techniques of lathework will not be discussed here. Several good introductory books are available to cover wood turning, metal turning, and spinning.

A small, high-speed hand grinder such as the Dremel Moto-Tool is very valuable for shaping small parts, smoothing the inside of finger holes, and polishing brass or ivory.

Sources of Designs

The instruments described in this book are only a beginning. They have been chosen to illustrate techniques that can then be applied to all sorts of other instruments. There are a number of beautifully illustrated books about historical musical instruments. The instrument maker will want to examine those that are available in libraries and perhaps to buy some. A list of such books is given in the Bibliography. Of the general books *Ancient European Musical Instruments*, by N. Bessaraboff is most useful to the craftsman, because it gives careful measurements of all instruments. The *Encyclopaedia Britannica* (11th ed.) has excellent articles on musical instruments, and the plates on instrument construction in Diderot's great French *L'Encyclopédie* are gorgeous (they may be found under "Lutherie" and "Chaudronnier"). A complete facsimile edition of *L'Encyclopédie* is available now in major libraries. The selection of plates from the facsimile edition of *L'Encyclopédie* published by Dover does not include most of the instrument plates.

The Galpin Society concerns itself with the study of ancient instruments. The instrument maker may want to join this group, and he certainly should become acquainted with the *Galpin Society Journal* where detailed articles on all types of instruments are published regularly. The present secretary of the Galpin Society is Dr. Maurice Byrne, School of Physics, University of Warwick, Coventry CV4 7AL, England.

The only book to give much detail about current techniques of instrument construction is *The Making of Musical Instruments* by T. C. Young. There is an excellent series of articles entitled "Woodwind Instruments" by P. Tomlin in *Woodworker* in which directions are given for making several woodwind instruments. E. D. Brand's book on instrument repairing, *Band Instrument Repairing Manual*, while it does not describe instrument making from scratch, is very valuable for its descriptions of many useful techniques.

Books are fine so far as they go, but there is no substitute for seeing, handling, and measuring actual instruments. While some nineteenth-century instruments can still be found at reasonable prices in antique shops, the ancient instruments that the craftsman will be most interested in copying are either sold at very high prices by specialists or are in museum collections. The wind instrument collections in the United States that are most readily available for observation and, by permission, examination and measurement are those at the Smithsonian Institution and the Library of Congress, Washington D.C.; the Metropolitan Museum of Art, New York; the Museum of Fine Arts, Boston; and the University of Michigan, Ann Arbor. In Europe there are major collections at Brussels, Berlin, and Munich and in other large cities. Bessaraboff's *Ancient European Musical Instruments* is based on the Boston collection and is in fact a much elaborated catalog. A checklist of the Dayton Miller Collection in the Library of Congress is also available, and a similar list for wind instruments at the Smithsonian is in preparation. Catalogs of the other major collections were published many years ago and are now out of print, although it may be possible to find them in some libraries. A listing of collections is given in Appendix A. A complete directory of both public and private collections is currently being prepared for publication under the auspices of UNESCO.

Additional instrument drawings may also be obtained from me.

Pitch and Tuning

The subject of proper pitch can become extremely complicated as anyone who consults standard musical encyclopedias or Bessaraboff's book on instruments will discover. My purpose here is to give just a few helpful hints to the craftsman.

The presently accepted evenly tempered musical scale exemplified by the piano keyboard is about two hundred years old, and instruments made before that time will have slightly different intervals between notes. Most old woodwind instruments used compromised tunings that were adjusted by forked fingerings, and these tunings were made to favor certain keys (e.g., F for recorders; D for flutes). Purists may wish to duplicate the old uneven tunings, and many will insist that old music sounds better when played as its composer heard it. However, most reproductions of old instruments are given modern tuning.

The basic pitch of instruments has also undergone change over the years. That is, the sound that today we call C might in earlier times have been called C-sharp or D. A result of this is that when an exact reproduction of an old instrument is made, it cannot be played along with modern instruments unless the player transposes keys. The pitch of orchestral instruments from about 1600 to 1800 was a half tone below modern pitch (their C is our B) and is called *Hoch Kammerton*. In contrast, outdoor band musicians tuned their instruments a full tone higher than modern pitch (their C is our D). As with the division of the scale, then, the pitch becomes a problem for the instrument maker, who must choose between making an exact reproduction of an old instrument or making an instrument that resembles it but is pitched like a modern instrument. If the latter course is to be followed, the dimensions of the old instrument will have to be adjusted. For example, to raise the pitch of a baroque flute by a half tone the length must be shortened by about $1\frac{1}{2}$ in. and all the finger holes must be moved up. The result will be an instrument that possesses many characteristics of its prototype; but it cannot strictly be called a replica, for notes of identical pitch played on the two instruments will differ in tone quality and strength.

In this book I take no position on the issue of exact replica versus somewhat modified "antique types" of instruments. The techniques that are described are obviously generally applicable to either. Some of the designs given are for exact replicas, and reference is made to their prototypes; others I have modified somewhat. The craftsman is advised to let musicians and musicologists argue and get on with his work, realizing that there are many degrees of accuracy, and that in this business *absolute* fidelity to an original is unattainable.

The amateur will probably not wish to invest in electronic standards for tuning and will rely on aural comparisons. As primary standards, tuning forks of several pitches can be obtained. The intensity of sound from a tuning fork can be strengthened by mounting it on a simple resonator box (fig. 1). A pitch pipe, well-tuned piano, or other commercial instrument is also valuable when adjusting the notes not covered by the tuning forks.

Two commonly accepted notations for designation of octaves are illustrated below.

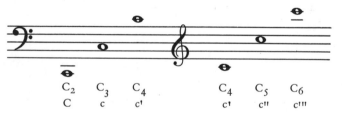

Thus the note on the middle line of the treble staff can be referred to unambiguously as b′, or the range of a tenor recorder described as C_4 through C_6.

Measurements

For anyone who has taken time to become familiar with it, the metric system is far easier to use; and all measurements in such

FIGURE I. Tuning fork on resonator.

books as Bessaraboff's are given in the metric system. Still, the English system lingers on, and I have been reluctant to discard it completely. A trumpet 7 ft. long seems to be more readily visualized than one which is 2,128 mm. in length. However, for measurement of finger holes and trumpet mouthpieces the metric system seems far superior. To assist the craftsman whose calipers and drills may be gauged according to the English system, Appendix D is a conversion table. The figures throughout the book give dimensions in millimeters, with the background ruling in inches.

Anyone who consults old books that give measurements of instruments will encounter some other measurement systems. In French small dimensions may be measured in *lignes* with 12 *lignes* to the *pouce*. The *pouce* is 1.0658 in., so the *ligne* is 2.25 mm. or slightly more than $\frac{1}{12}$ in. German writers, such as Praetorius, give measurements in Brunswick feet. The Brunswick foot equals 0.94 of a modern foot and was divided into 12 in., so that a Brunswick inch equals 0.94 of a modern inch or 23.78 mm.

2
Wooden Instruments
Materials and Methods

The subject matter of this chapter is chosen from the point of view of manufacturing methods rather than from that of acoustics because, for example, cornetti are acoustically "brass" instruments although made of wood. It is a surprise to most people that the construction material is not of major importance in controlling the characteristic sound of an instrument. The importance lies not in the material itself but in the different results of machining. For instance, the harder the material, the sharper the corners may be at the edges of joints and finger holes. V. C. Mahillon in his classic *Éléments d'Acoustique* (pp. 63–65) tells of making a cavalry bugle of standard dimensions from wood and being unable to distinguish its timbre from that of a brass instrument. This story, though, is doubted by modern scholars of musical instruments.

Choice of Wood

As mentioned above, the choice of wood for instrument construction is based more on consideration of mechanical properties and appearance than consideration of acoustic properties. Hard, fine-grained woods are preferred, because they can be machined with greater precision than soft woods and have greater dimensional stability. Woods that have a tendency to swell or warp are generally to be avoided, although modern penetrating finishes for wood are quite successful in preventing absorption of moisture. The instrument maker should not have to be much concerned with the proper seasoning of wood, since a reputable dealer will have seen to it that the wood he sells is ready for working. However, it is always a good idea to put wood aside for a while at the humidity where it will be used and to notice if any twisting or cracking appears. It is a heartbreaking disaster to see a finished instrument ruined by movement of the wood.

Occasionally you may want to season your own wood if, for example, you can acquire orchard trees at little or no cost. After cutting the wood roughly to size, paint the end grain with paraffin or tar, and stack the pieces in an unheated building or outside to allow circulation of air around them (but cover them to keep off rain and snow). About one year of seasoning for each inch of thickness is usually recommended, and after this time another year in a heated building is a good idea. Carefully managed kiln drying can speed up this process, but it is not an operation for the amateur to undertake. Another useful procedure that has recently become available for stabilization of wood is to immerse the green pieces in a 30% to 40% (by weight) aqueous solution of polyethylene glycol 1000 (available from dealers in industrial chemicals). After two or three months in this solution allow the wood to dry for a few more months, and it will not undergo any further shrinking. With this treatment instruments may be made out of branches in the round that would surely split if simply seasoned in the usual way.

Boxwood (*Buxus sempervirens* and *B. balearica*) was for many years the favorite wood for making flutes, recorders, oboes, and clarinets; as it was the hardest, finest grained wood that was readily available in Europe. Its disadvantage was a pronounced tendency to warp, and bent boxwood instruments can be seen in any large collection of old instruments. The purist who is determined to make exact reproductions of old instruments will want to try boxwood, but it is practically unobtainable in large enough dimensions nowadays. Some possible sources are listed in Appendix B.

Traditionally, boxwood was seasoned by burying it in the ground for something like twenty years, but I have used boxwood without such seasoning and have not observed any distortion or cracking in the finished wood. The undistinguished color of new boxwood is a disappointment in comparison to the rich orange yellow of old instruments. The old makers sometimes colored boxwood by treating it with chemicals such as nitric acid. Deep staining with the usual wood stains is not possible because of the hardness of the wood, but a pretty good approximation is possible.

Because of the shortage of genuine boxwood, other species have been introduced into the trade to replace it. Only one of these, the Cape, or East London Boxwood (*Buxus macowami*) from

Africa, is botanically a true boxwood. Also from Africa is Knysna boxwood or kamassi (*Gonioma kamassi*). West Indian boxwood or zapatero seems to come from a confusing number of species that are lumped together under this name, including species of *Phyllostylon, Gossypiospermum, Tecoma, Casearia*, and *Aspidosperma*. There is general agreement that none of these substitutes is as good as genuine boxwood, but that they may be the best available.

If the wooden instrument business had developed in North America rather than Europe, it seems likely that the commonly used wood might have been hard maple (*Acer saccharum*). It is not so dense as boxwood and is also adversely affected by moisture, but it has a fine grain and machines well. As with boxwood, its uninteresting color can be improved by light staining. Its low cost recommends it for experimentation, and its availability in quite large dimensions (e.g., 4 in. × 4 in. squares) makes it almost the only wood that can be used for some instruments.

Among the other native North American woods the fruit woods apple, cherry, and pear are most useful to the instrument maker. Of these only cherry is usually available commercially, but apple and pear may be obtained from orchardists who are removing old trees or by finding abandoned trees that are fairly common around old communities. Birch is rather similar to maple in its characteristics but is usually slightly softer. Some European recorders are made of birch, but I would not consider it as a first choice. American black walnut is a beautiful wood to look at and to work with. It is softer than hard maple, though, and is rather coarse grained so that filler may have to be used for a smooth surface. Despite these disadvantages walnut seems to be the ideal wood for krumhorns because of the ease with which it can be bent.

During the nineteenth century, tropical woods gradually re-placed northern woods in the making of instruments. Not only were some very hard woods available from the tropics, but many of them showed beautiful colors and figures. The naming of these tropical woods has been extremely confusing. Sometimes two or more names have been applied to the same wood; sometimes different woods have been called by the same or similar name. I have tabulated some of these woods below giving first the botanical names, which alone are free from ambiguity. The reader interested in learning more about these woods will want to consult the following valuable books: *World Timbers*, by B. J. Rendle; *Timbers for Woodwork*, by J. C. S. Brough; *What Wood is That?*, by H. L. Edlin; *Know Your Woods*, by A. Constantine, Jr.; and *Fine Hardwoods Selectorama*, published by the Fine Hardwoods Association.

Brya ebenus, green ebony, cocus wood. A dark brown, hard, and heavy wood obtained mostly from the West Indies. Not readily available.

Caesalpinia granadillo, brown ebony, granadillo. Very similar to the above and sometimes confused with it. Also from the West Indies and not readily available.

Diospyros ebenum, ebony. This species is the original ebony obtained from India and Ceylon. Other species of *Diospyros* are also called ebony and include *D. celebica* or Macassar ebony, *D. dendo* or Gaboon ebony, and *D. marmorata* or marble wood. To add to the confusion some entirely unrelated trees are called ebony only because they have dark-colored wood. Ebony is not generally used now for construction of complete instruments since it does not have good dimensional stability although it is valuable for mouthpieces or decorations. All dealers in rare woods stock some kind of ebony.

Dalbergia retusa, cocobolo. A hard, heavy wood of reddish orange color. It is difficult to work but gives a beautiful end result. Some people are allergic to cocobolo, and no one should acquire an instrument made of it without being tested by exposure to it. Cocobolo is available from all dealers in rare woods.

Dalbergia nigra, Brazilian rosewood, rio jacaranda, palisander. A beautiful, heavy wood ranging in color from a rather bright red to a deep reddish brown, with black streaks. Although somewhat brittle, rosewood makes excellent instruments and is readily obtained from dealers in imported woods. Other so-called rosewoods are available, for instance *Dalbergia stevensonii* or Honduras rosewood, *Dalbergia latifolia* or East Indian rosewood, and *Guibourtia demeusii* or bubinga or African rosewood. All have the reddish color of rosewood but do not have the strongly contrasting black streaks of the Brazilian species.

Dalbergia melanoxylon, African blackwood, grenadilla. Although related to the rosewoods this wood is so dark as to resemble the ebonies. It is very scarce but is traditionally used for clarinets, oboes, and Highland bagpipes.

Peltogyne pubescens, purpleheart, amaranth. Obtained from the West Indies and South America, this wood is readily available and unique for its rich purple color.

Pterocarpus dalbergiodes, padouk, padauk, vermilion, Andaman redwood. A heavy, hard wood of a striking red color. It has a rather coarse grain that may need filling. It is available from most dealers in imported woods.

Dalbergia oliveri, *D. variabilis*, tulip wood, Bahia rosewood. A hard wood of density similar to *Dalbergia nigra* but with a striking figure contrasting rich purple with cream color. With age the color tends to fade.

Boring and Reaming

Boring is the first step in making any wooden instrument. When the bore has been completed, the piece is held between conical centers for turning the exterior. In this way the exterior will be concentric with the bore even if the boring has not gone perfectly straight.

The average woodworking shop is not likely to be equipped for the type of boring that is necessary in making instruments. Acquisition of suitable tools for this operation is likely to be the most expensive and time-consuming aspect of getting started in the instrument making business. Cylindrical bores up to 8 in. or 9 in. long and $\frac{3}{8}$ in. to 1 in. in diameter can be made with ordinary spade bits and an extension shank. With luck it is even possible to drill from both ends and meet in the middle for holes of this length. With longer holes the tendency to drift to the side becomes too great, and twist drills are even worse in this respect. Acquisition of a set of Ridgway shell augers is the key to successful long hole boring. These augers are available in sizes of $\frac{1}{4}$ in. to $\frac{1}{2}$ in. in increments of $\frac{1}{16}$ in., and lengths of 12 in. to 36 in. in increments of 6 in. When used for very long holes the $\frac{1}{4}$-in. size shows some tendency to wander, especially if it is not kept very sharp; but it can be controlled by going slowly and clearing chips frequently. The bigger sizes are perfectly reliable for drilling straight holes up to their maximum length. Once a straight hole has been drilled with one of these augers, it can easily be enlarged by running a twist drill or a homemade flat-tipped drill of the desired size through it. Therefore it is not necessary to acquire the Ridgway augers in all diameters. The setup for boring with these augers requires a hollow dead center in the lathe through which the auger is inserted. This center can be made easily from a $\frac{1}{2}$-in. bronze water pipe tee. One end of the tee is beveled to a sharp edge, and a length of pipe attached to the side outlet can be held in the usual tool rest holder. Shallow $\frac{5}{8}$-in. holes are drilled in the centers of the wood to be bored. One end is turned at the live center by a chuck or dog, while the other is supported by the hollow center through which the auger is fed. A speed of about 1,000 rpm is satisfactory for this boring, and the auger must be withdrawn frequently to clear chips. The wood should be reversed before boring all the way through so that the tip of the auger is not damaged by running onto the live center. A crafts-man handy in blacksmithing can make a reasonable facsimile of the Ridgway augers, but at their price it is hardly worth the effort. Instructions are given in Appendix C.

Except for krumhorns, clarinets, and racketts, the wooden in-struments described in this book have a conical rather than a cylindrical bore. Special tools are available in the industry for boring conical holes in a single operation, but for the small-scale craftsman the easiest approach is to bore a cylindrical hole first and then ream it to the required conical shape. Standard machinists' taper pin reamers come in a wide range of diameters all with a taper of $1:48$ ($\frac{1}{4}$ in. per foot). This happens to be just about right for recorders and several other instruments, so that acquisition of several of these reamers is desirable. However in the larger sizes they can be quite expensive (some sources of used and low-priced surplus reamers are listed in Appendix B). To decrease the expense and to obtain reamers in nonstandard tapers, it is necessary for the craftsman to make his own.

Steel-fluted reamers are made by first turning a rod to the required taper, then milling or grinding grooves along it, and finally sharpening and relieving the cutting edges. An abrasive disc mounted in the tool post grinder can be used for cutting grooves while the reamer is mounted in the lathe (see fig. 2). Another approach is to make a vee block with its base slanted, so that when the reamer blank is placed into the vee its top surface is level. An abrasive disc mounted on a radial saw can then be passed over and successively lowered to grind out the grooves. For cutting wood it is not necessary to use tool steel or to harden the cutting edges. A reamer that has been recommended to me by two instrument makers, but which I have never tried, is made by milling a single deep groove so that in cross-section a 90° sector is removed from the cone. Then one corner is raised above the surface with a burnisher and honed to a sharp edge.

For larger diameter reamers (i.e., $\frac{3}{4}$ in. at the small end) the body of the reamer can be turned from hard wood to the correct taper and the cutting edges inserted into slots sawed into the wood. Old hacksaw blades are good for this purpose. The slots should be sawed carefully to expose about $\frac{1}{16}$ in. of the inserted blade. The blades are held in place by cutting grooves around the wood to match holes drilled through the blades (after heating to draw the temper). Wire pulled through the holes and around the grooves is twisted together, and any spaces along the blades are filled with epoxy cement. The protruding edges of the blades are finally ground to a sharp, beveled edge.

FIGURE 2. Making a tapered reamer.

The easiest reamer to make is a flat one ground from a file to have the required taper and sharpened to a slight bevel along the edges. Such a reamer has to be guided slowly and carefully, but if it is well made it will do a surprisingly smooth job.

It is a temptation to try driving the reamer with an electric drill to hasten the process, but it is not really that much faster than turning by hand if the reamer is sharp, and slow cutting seems to give a smoother finish. The three types of homemade reamers described are illustrated in figure 3.

If very precise measurements are taken of the bores of old instruments, it will usually be found that they are not perfectly uniform cones or cylinders but have some abrupt steps in diameter. While these steps are not large in any absolute sense—less than half a millimeter over a distance of one or two centimeters—they may have important influence on tone and pitch. A. Baines, in *Woodwind Instruments* (p. 277), believes that some of these irregular profiles are to be regarded as "primitive" rather than the result of "deliberate experiment in pursuit of musical objectives." However, the musical effects are by no means negligible. A. H. Benade has told me about "transforming" instruments by adding or subtracting as little as 0.005 in. from selected places in the bore. This observation points out again, though, the dilemma facing anyone who is a perfectionist in pursuing exact replication of old instruments: whether to copy irregularities precisely, or make an average, uniform cone.

Joints

The earliest woodwind instruments were made of single pieces of wood (e.g., Renaissance recorders and shawms), but towards the end of the seventeenth century it became customary to make instruments with several detachable tenon and socket joints. The bore can be made with greater ease and accuracy in a short length, and the resulting instrument is more convenient to carry. These advantages outweigh the increased fragility and the work of making the joints.

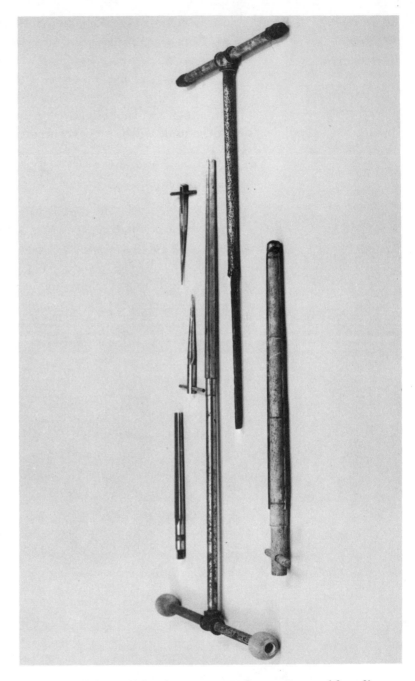

FIGURE 3. *Left*, four steel-fluted reamers; *center*, flat reamer ground from file; *right*, wooden bodied reamer.

The socket is more likely to be concentric with the bore if it is bored first in the end of the piece of wood, and then the smaller drill used for the rest of the bore; but when the long shell augers are used for the bore, it is easier to bore through the length first and then enlarge the socket end with a larger drill. A slight lack of concentricity will not be noticed in the assembled instrument, since the outside will be turned concentric with the socket rather than with the main bore. For strength, the wall of the instrument should be thickened around the socket or a ferrule added. Another useful trick for minimizing strain on the socket is to bore about the first $\frac{1}{8}$ in. just slightly larger than the rest of the socket. In this way when the joint is assembled, the wedging pressure of the tenon is not exerted on the fragile edge of the socket where cracks are most likely to start.

Tenons are turned after the rest of the exterior of the instrument so that their thin walls will not be cracked during the turning of the other parts. In the earliest instruments, joints were made tight by wrapping the tenons with waxed thread. If this method is to be used, the fit between tenon and socket should be quite close so that only a few layers of thread are needed. Figure 4 shows how the thread is wrapped. A rather soft, fuzzy thread rubbed with cork grease is best for this purpose. Suitable stuff is called *lapping thread* by instrument makers. The hemp used for bagpipe stocks is also satisfactory. Modern instruments use cork on the tenons. To apply this the tenon should be turned about $\frac{1}{16}$ in. smaller in diameter than the socket, and then an additional wide, shallow groove should be made to keep the cork band from any tendency to slide off. A strip of $\frac{1}{16}$ in. thick cork is cut the width of the groove, beveled at the ends to fit, and glued in place with contact cement or white glue. Careful sandpapering or filing will bring the cork down to a tight fit in the socket, and application of a little grease after the instrument is finished will make the fit just right. Sheets of ground cork composition and sheets of natural cork are both available from instrument repair shops. The former are much cheaper and tougher; but the latter, being softer and more resilient, make for a tighter joint.

Ferrules, Bushings, Decorations

Various parts of instruments devised originally for practical reasons can also be valued for their ornamental effects. The ivory rings around the joints of old instruments were probably intended to strengthen these joints, but in many cases it can be seen that it is the ivory that has cracked while the wood underneath remains whole. Still, ivory rings add a lot to the appearance of a fine instrument and are not overly expensive or difficult to make. The general procedure is to take a cross-sectional slice from a tusk and, using a drill or hole saw, cut the inner diameter to a snug fit on the wooden instrument and the other diameter somewhat larger than the finished outer diameter. A groove should then be cut around the inside of the ring and a matching groove cut around the outside of the instrument. The grooves can be made on the lathe or freehand with a high-speed hand grinder. Both grooves are filled with epoxy cement and the ring pressed on. In this way a ring of epoxy surrounds the instrument underneath the ivory ring, and it is the epoxy that really does the strengthening job. When the cement has hardened, the instrument is returned to the lathe for final shaping of the exterior, including the ivory ring. Ivory cuts easily with sharp wood-turning tools and should be finally buffed to a shiny finish using Tripoli compound on a cotton wheel. The wood underneath an ivory ring should be kept thin so that when it swells it will be less likely to crack the ivory.

Bushings of ivory on the inside of tone holes are also pretty; and in cases where a hole has accidentally been made too big, the mistake can not only be saved by inserting a bushing, but the instrument may even look better for it. The embouchure hole of old flutes was often bushed with ivory in order to present a hard, stable surface. To make bushings, thin discs of ivory are cut out with a plug cutter. The hole in the instrument is made to fit the disc, and the ivory is fastened into place with epoxy or contact cement. When the cement has hardened, a new hole of the right size can be drilled through the ivory.

Other materials can be substituted for ivory. Ordinary beef bones, if polished, are hard to distinguish from ivory at a distance, although they lack the characteristic grain pattern of ivory; and pieces suitable for making large rings, such as around the bell of an oboe, are not available. Fresh beef bones should be cleaned and aged for several months by burying them in the ground. A faster procedure used by old makers of bone implements was to steep the cut bones in a 1 % brine solution for three or four days, and then simmer it in water for about six hours. Plastics can of course be substituted for the natural materials; but their uniform color and texture makes them less attractive than ivory or bone. The best plastic to use is hard nylon. It is very strong, machines well, and has a color like that of ivory. Nylon pipe fittings are available from dealers in plumbing supplies and may be cut off to provide rings nearly ready for use.

For real strength brass ferrules are preferred. They are cut with a tubing cutter from brass tubing. Various sizes of brass tubing are available from plumbing shops. Some is chrome plated but can be used after sanding off the chrome.

Keys

Most of the instruments that the amateur will make will not require keys, and even those that do have only one or two. Most common are closed keys that open a hole when the lever is pressed. Open keys, in contrast, close a hole when operated and are used at the lower end of the oboe and larger recorders to obtain the lowest notes of these instruments. The general forms of the two mechanisms are illustrated in figure 5. The key is shaped from $\frac{1}{16}$-in. brass sheet by sawing, filing, and hammering it against a lead anvil. Brass that is too soft can be stiffened by preliminary cold working with the hammer. The pivot bearing can be made by leaving projections at the sides of the key, bending them down at right angles and drilling holes through them; or a shallow, rounded groove can be filed across the underside of the key and a length of fine brass tubing silver-soldered into it. Springs are made of thin spring brass or steel that should be riveted and not just soldered to the key. Small brass escutcheon pins make excellent rivets for this purpose. Some makers have used helical springs fitted into sockets on the underside of the key and on the top of the instrument. This is not the traditional method, but it gives satisfactory results. In the oldest instruments the key fastening was made by leaving a ring turned around the instrument, cutting a channel through it for the key, and running the axle through holes drilled across the channel. In later instruments much of the ring was cut away to leave just two wooden posts supporting the axle. Finally, inserted metal posts came into common use to support the axle. Pads on early instruments were made of soft leather; if suitable leather can be obtained it is quite satisfactory. The pad can be attached to the key by roughening the metal surface and using contact cement. A flat, smooth surface must be made around the hole that is to be closed. A slightly raised rim around the hole may make for a better air seal, but it was not usually present on old instruments.

Reeds

Making reeds is a complex and difficult art requiring much practice and specialized tools. In general the amateur instrument maker is advised to buy his reeds ready-made or to get lessons from an expert. I make an exception to this principle in the case of krumhorn and rackett reeds because the requirements for these reeds are less exacting; and commercial reeds, while available with difficulty, are exorbitantly priced.

Placement of Finger Holes

It comes as a surprise to many that there is a certain amount of
latitude possible in the placement of finger holes. In general
there are three main goals to be satisfied, and the final hole positions and sizes reflect a compromise among them. (1) An inconvenient reach for the fingers should be avoided. To accommodate
a player with small hands it may be possible to move the holes
closer together or to move the holes for the third and fourth fingers
out of line with the other holes. (2) The volume of sound coming
from a hole is controlled by the size of the hole so that for all
notes to be of equal loudness, holes should be of nearly the same
size. (3) Control of pitch is, of course, the primary consideration;
the rule of thumb is that a small hole nearer the mouthpiece will
give the same pitch as a larger hole farther down. Thus if a hole
is to be moved up to satisfy the first goal, it must also be made
smaller. If it is enlarged to satisfy the second goal, it must be
moved down. The place where the hole meets the air column on
the inside is what controls the pitch, so that in a thick-walled
instrument the finger holes may be drilled at an angle to make
them closer together on the outside than they are on the inside.
Where double holes are used to make it easier to play chromatics,
it is useful to slant the lower note hole toward the bottom of the
instrument and the higher one toward the top. The wall thickness
of the instrument will also affect the pitch, because the length
of the air column is increased by the length of the open finger
hole. Since closed holes also contribute to the volume of the bore,
big finger holes have more of an effect on the pitch issuing from
lower holes (flattening it) than small holes do.

With the foregoing considerations in mind the procedure for
making the finger holes follows logically. Approximate hole
positions are decided on, and small holes are drilled. Then,
starting with the lowest note, each note is tuned to a standard by
sounding the instrument and enlarging the hole until it sounds the
right pitch. After boring all the holes by this procedure the

bottom notes will be flat, because the effect of closed upper holes is not the same as an unbroken bore. The lower holes must therefore be enlarged, and the correct tuning approached by successive approximations always working from the bottom up. Even when copying other instruments or following the designs in this book, it is wise to start by making the finger holes smaller than the given measurements and then gradually enlarge them until the right pitch is achieved.

Finish

The finish to be applied to the wood is largely a matter of personal taste unless one desires to make an exact replica of some historical instrument. A penetrating finish should be applied to the bore of wooden instruments as a seal against moisture. One end can be plugged with a cork, finger holes closed with masking tape, and the tube filled with finish and allowed to drain after a time. The outside can be stained if desired, then finished with either a varnish or a penetrating oil finish such as Firzite, and finally waxed. Polyurethane varnish thinned 1:1 makes a good first coat for both bore and exterior since it will penetrate well. Later coats can be thinned less. Before applying the interior finish and after each application is hard, the bore should be given a smooth, hard surface. The tool for this internal smoothing is simply a dowel with a saw kerf in the end to hold a strip of abrasive cloth that is wrapped around it. The dowel is then turned in a drill press at 1,000 to 2,000 rpm while the instrument is worked back and forth over the abrasive. Finally a slight chamfer should be made on the inside edge of each finger hole. Such chamfering improves the loudness and dynamic range by effectively smoothing the bore.

Metal or ivory parts are smoothed with a rubber-bonded fine abrasive wheel and finally buffed with Tripoli compound on a cloth wheel.

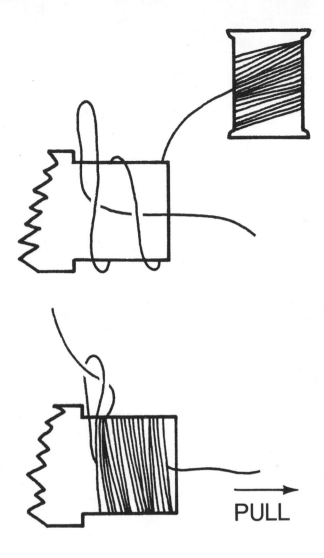

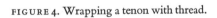
PULL

FIGURE 4. Wrapping a tenon with thread.

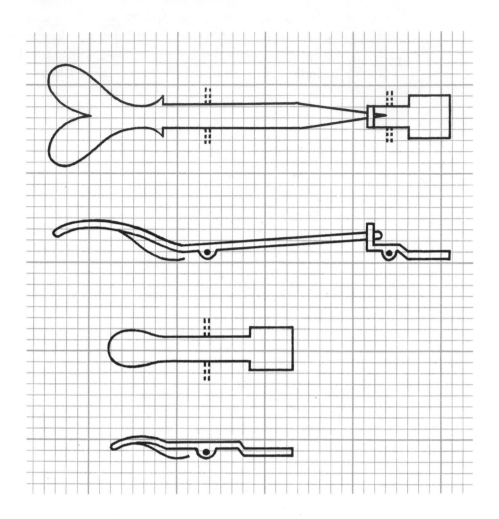

FIGURE 5. Key designs, top and side views: *above*, open key; *below*, closed key.

3
Flute and Fife

The fife is probably the simplest to make of all the instruments described in this book, since it is one piece with a completely cylindrical bore. Dimensions are given here for fifes in C and in B-flat (fig. 7, table 3.1). The lowest note is theoretically c″ or b-flat′, but the lowest two or three notes are weak, and it is a much more effective instrument in its upper range. For positioning the cork plug, see the discussion below regarding the flute.

The one-keyed flute in D of a design like the one presented here (fig. 8, table 3.2) came into use at the end of the seventeenth century. Before this time transverse flutes were keyless and had a cylindrical rather than a conical bore. During the eighteenth century additional keys were added until, at the beginning of the nineteenth century, flutes with six, seven, or eight keys were in use.

The chief problem in making a conically bored flute is getting suitable reamers. These must be made, since the necessary taper is much more gradual than can be found in commercially available reamers of such diameter. It is tempting to try to compromise, such as by making the cylindrical section longer and then tapering more abruptly with a $\frac{1}{4}$ in. to the foot reamer, but experience shows that this creates a flute in which it is almost impossible to get the low and high registers in tune with each other. The diameters must also be adhered to quite strictly (at least not increased), or the result will be, again, a flute in which either the high or the low register can be brought into tune but not both together. The embouchure hole on many old flutes was undercut, that is, the diameter increased as it approached the bore. Undercutting facilitates production of high notes but reduces the power of the lowest octave. A very *slight* chamfering of the outer edge is considered desirable.

Placement of the cork is an operation peculiar to tuning the flute (and fife). The rule of thumb is to locate the cork as a first approximation at a distance back from the center of the embouchure equal to the diameter of the bore at this point. The lowest note (d′ on the flute) is hardly sensitive to cork position and can be tuned by cutting off the lower end of the instrument if required.

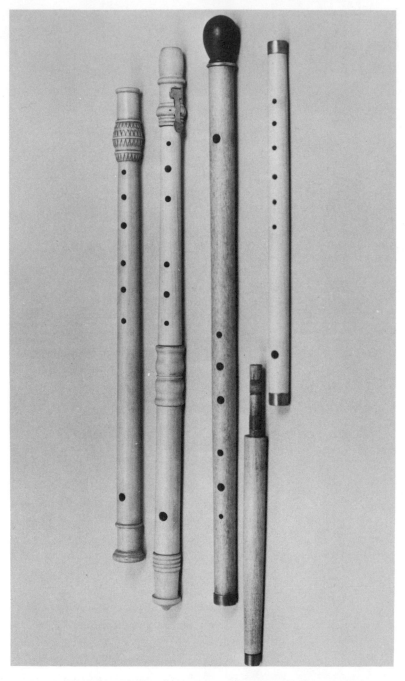

FIGURE 6. *From left to right*, Renaissance type of flute, baroque flute, walking stick flute, and fife.

When this is satisfactory, the cork is moved until the octave (d″) can be overblown accurately. Moving the cork toward the embouchure sharpens the overblown note, and moving it away flattens it. When the cork has been located so that the octave is in tune, the note holes can be drilled and adjusted to give the intervening tones. For final tuning it is best to adjust so that the octave overblows most accurately at G. This gives the best compromise for other notes. Notes in the upper octave are apparently more sensitive to hole diameter than notes in the lower; so if the lower note is in tune, but its octave is flat, the note hole can be enlarged enough to sharpen the octave without noticeably sharpening the fundamental.

The walking stick flute (see fig. 9) was a nineteenth-century novelty. The simple design of the flute part makes it resemble flutes of a much earlier period. Some walking stick flutes did have keys, but they would have been awkward if the instrument was, in fact, used as a walking stick. The only constructional difficulty worthy of mention is the result of the flute section being unjointed. This necessitates adding extensions to the reamers for the boring operation. The bottom end of the flute needs to have a cylindrical bore for proper fitting of the foot section, and the upper end must allow for enough space above the cork for insertion of the handle.

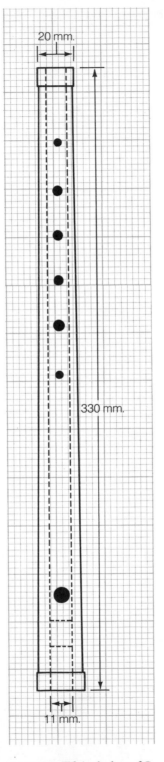

FIGURE 7. Fife in the key of C.

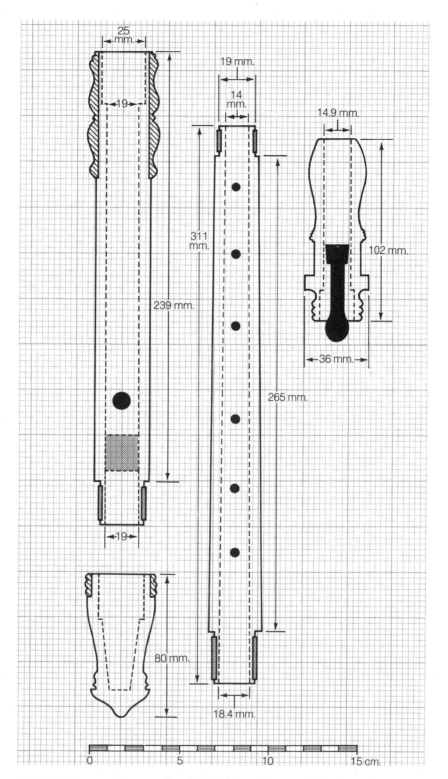

FIGURE 8. A copy of a baroque flute in the Boston Museum of Fine Arts collection (no. 38). The original is made of boxwood with ivory rings.

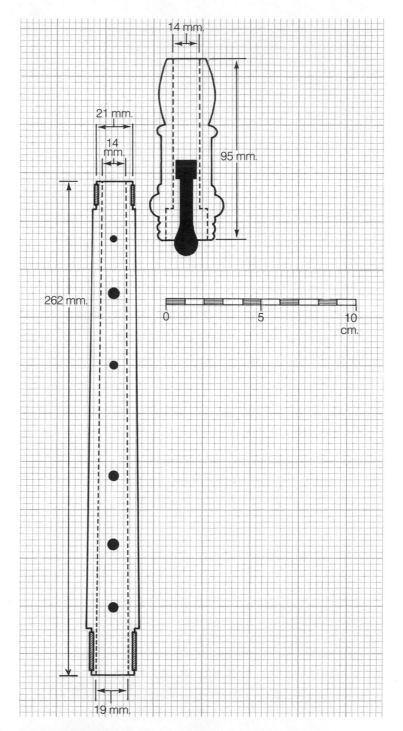

FIGURE 8. Modified joints which will bring the instrument up a
semitone to modern pitch.

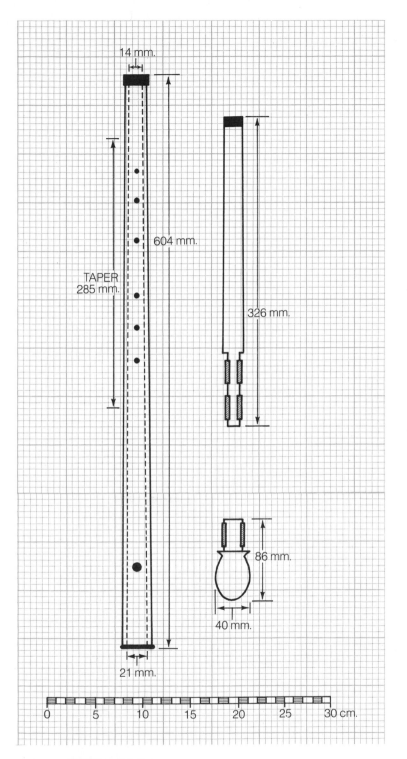

14 mm.

604 mm.

TAPER
285 mm.

21 mm.

326 mm.

86 mm.

40 mm.

0   5   10   15   20   25   30 cm.

FIGURE 9. Walking stick flute.

TABLE 3.1

Fife Hole Dimensions

Finger hole distances measured from center of embouchure hole to centers of finger holes.

Hole Number	B-Flat Fife		C Fife	
	Distance (mm.)	Diameter (mm.)	Distance (mm.)	Diameter (mm.)
Embouchure	0	8.5	0	8.5
1	142	4.0	115	4.5
2	167	5.5	142	6.0
3	191	5.0	167	6.0
4	215	3.0	190	5.5
5	238	4.5	214	5.5
6	261	4.0	238	4.5
Bottom	325	11.0	295	11.0

TABLE 3.2
Flute Hole Dimensions

Finger hole distances measured from center of embouchure hole to centers of finger holes.

Hole Number	Original		Modern Pitch	
	Distance (mm.)	Diameter (mm.)	Distance (mm.)	Diameter (mm.)
Embouchure	0	9.8 × 9.3	0	9.0
1	239	7.0	216	6.5
2	274	7.0	257	7.5
3	313	6.0	288	8.0
4	365	6.0	347	6.5
5	405	5.8	385	7.5
6	442	5.0	417	5.0
7	497	6.0	462	6.0

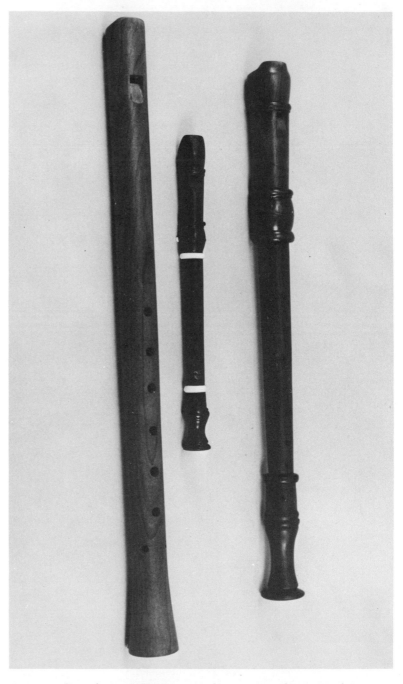

FIGURE 10. Recorders: *Left*, Renaissance-style tenor; *center*, baroque-style soprano; *right*, baroque-style tenor.

4
Recorders

The recorder achieved nearly its modern form as early as the fourteenth century and continues even today to be a popular instrument with amateur players because of the relative ease with which it can be played. However, in the hands of a virtuoso, it can be an impressive instrument. Six sizes of recorder are well recognized ranging from sopranino to great bass. The lower pitched instruments often suffer from weak sound, and there is little music written for the shrill sopranino. The alto recorder is probably most popular because of its relative loudness and the range it covers. In writing this chapter I am especially indebted to Arthur Benade who has given me the results of many experiments relating constructional modifications to acoustic results. A very useful article by R. Marvin, "Recorders and English Flutes in European Collections," gives precise measurements for fifteen important museum specimens of recorders.

The designs presented here for baroque recorders (figs. 10, 11, 12; table 4.1) follow traditional dimensions and styling, although they are in modern pitch. Recorders of the Renaissance period were generally made of a single piece of wood and had a bore with greater diameter and less taper (e.g., for the alto a maximum diameter of 21 mm. and a taper of 1 : 100). They also might have a slight flare of the same taper at the bell end starting at the seventh hole. Because of these differences the Renaissance recorders were louder in the lower octave but would not overblow for the full second octave.

The boring and turning operations for the middle and foot joints present no special problems. I have fixed on a taper of 1 : 48 ($\frac{1}{4}$ in. per foot) for recorders. This is in the range for baroque instruments and is convenient because of the availability of machinists' taper pin reamers that have this taper. For the soprano recorder, sizes no. 6 through no. 8 reamers are needed, for the alto sizes no. 9 through no. 11, and for the tenor sizes no. 10 through no. 12. Since the larger sizes are expensive, the amateur may wish to make wooden-bodied reamers as described in chapter 2.

The top joint is the crucial part of the recorder. Great precision is required in its construction, therefore the recorder is one of the most difficult instruments to make well. Step-by-step instructions are given as an aid in meeting some of the difficulties. A $\frac{1}{4}$-in. hole is first drilled straight through the piece. This serves to guide the larger bits for boring in order the socket joint, fipple bore, and main bore. The outside is then turned, being especially careful that the bottom edge of the ring just above the mouth coincides exactly with the bottom of the fipple bore. If a spade bit has been used for the fipple bore, the bottom will be flat; but if a twist drill has been used, the bottom will be chamfered toward the main bore, the fipple will have to be beveled to fit this chamfer, and the ring must be turned to coincide with the flat end of the fipple. When the outside turning is finished, the mouth is cut through by drilling and filing to a rectangular cross-section. The windway or flue is chiseled along the top of the fipple bore, removing just enough wood so that it is flat where it meets the mouth. The fipple should be turned of red cedar because of the moisture-resistant properties of this wood. When the diameter and length are right, a flat is filed along the top to match the chiseled wind-way, and a thin slip of cedar is glued to the flat to make a good seal with the bottom edge of the chiseled groove. When the fipple has been fitted so that its end coincides with the external ring and the windway opening at the mouth is the right size, the lip can be shaped by chiseling alternately from the outside and the inside so that the sharp edge comes slightly below the middle of the windway. This is achieved by sighting through the flue at the lip as the chiseling proceeds. During the chiseling it is a good idea to insert a slip of wood in the mouth so that the chisel does not strike the fipple or rear edge of the mouth. The relationship between lip and flue is crucial to a good recorder, and a slip in the chiseling is difficult to correct. Narrowing the flue from top to bottom makes the upper octave easier to play; but if it is too narrow, the lower octave becomes hard to play, and condensed moisture may obstruct the passage. Arched windways are made in some recorders and have an advantage in that condensed moisture runs to the edges, but the lip must also be curved so that its edge follows the center of the curved windway. Some of the best old instruments (e.g., those made by the Denners and the Stanesbys) have the top of the flue arched at the blowing end and gradually flattened out to give a rectangular section at the window end. Experiments by Benade have confirmed the value of shaping the flue in this way to smooth out the response, particularly for the lower notes. *Slight* chamfering at the window end of the flue is also helpful in brightening the tone and stabilizing the attack. No finish should be applied to the top of the fipple, because moisture tends to collect in large droplets on a finished surface rather than to spread out in a thin film. However, a penetrating finish applied to the fipple with thorough sanding between applications is of value. Benade has found that cutting away the underside of the fipple to create a cavity above the mouth helps to increase the dynamic range. Some Stanesby instruments were made this way. Since this modification also lowers the pitch, it cannot be simply applied to an instrument without also shortening the middle joint.

It appears that internal smoothness is more vital to the construction of the recorder than to that of any other instrument. In the main bore high polish, closely fitting joints with slightly chamfered and rounded ends, and slightly rounded edges on the finger holes make considerable improvement in the clarity of speech and smoothness over the whole range as well as increase the loudness of the low notes. A smooth flue is important throughout the range and can make an all-or-none difference in the highest notes.

The recorder designs given here are intended to be played with baroque fingering. For German fingering the fifth hole is made somewhat smaller so that the sixth hole does not have to be closed when playing F on the soprano and tenor or B-flat on the alto.

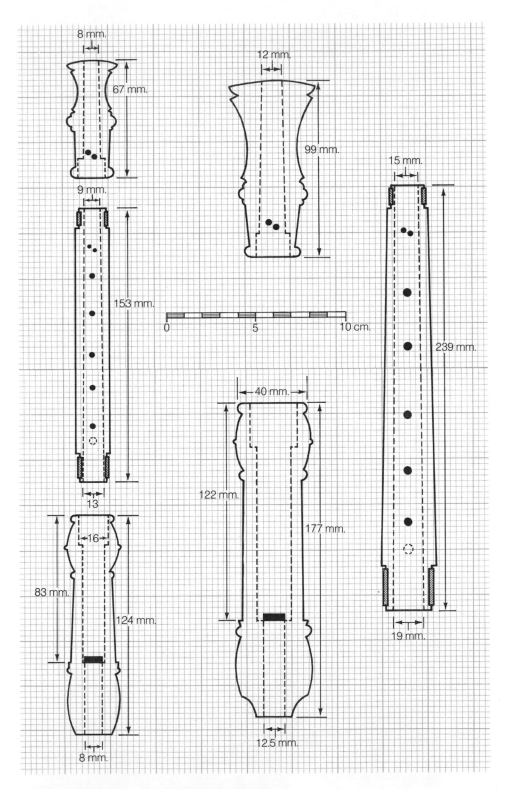

FIGURE II. *Left*, soprano recorder; *right*, alto recorder.

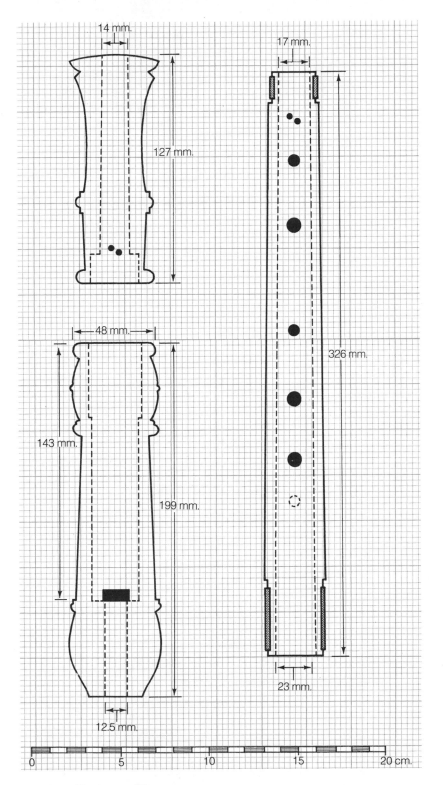

14 mm.

127 mm.

17 mm.

48 mm.

143 mm.

199 mm.

326 mm.

12.5 mm.

23 mm.

0   5   10   15   20 cm.

FIGURE 12. Tenor recorder.

TABLE 4.1

Recorder Finger Hole Dimensions

Finger hole distances measured from edge of lip to centers of finger holes.

Hole Number	Soprano Distance (mm.)	Diameter (mm.)	Alto Distance (mm.)	Diameter (mm.)	Tenor Distance (mm.)	Diameter (mm.)
Thumb	94	4.5	126	6.5	182	8.0
1	102	3.5	141	6.0	204	8.0
2	121	3.5	171	6.5	237	7.0
3	141	4.5	203	6.5	274	6.5
4	165	4.0	241	6.5	334	8.5
5	185	4.5	273	6.0	367	7.5
6A	200	2.5	304	2.5	392	4.0
6B	202	2.0	307	2.0	394	3.0
7A	227	2.5	335	2.5	421	3.5
7B	230	1.5	338	2.0	424	2.5

		Window Dimensions			
Width	Height	Width	Height	Width	Height
9.0	3.0	12.0	4.5	15.0	6.0

5
Clarinet

The invention of the forerunner of the modern clarinet has been credited to Cristoph Denner of Nuremberg at about the end of the seventeenth century; although, as with most instruments, more primitive ancestors can be traced back to an indefinite beginning. The instrument presented here (figs. 13 and 14, table 5.1) preserves the general appearance of Denner's earliest design, but it has been modified in three respects: the length has been shortened to bring it up to modern pitch; the third, fourth, and sixth finger holes are doubled to assist with playing chromatics (the seventh hole was already doubled by Denner); and the outer diameter of the mouthpiece has been increased so that a modern ligature will fit. Well into the nineteenth century, clarinet reeds were tied on with thread—a clumsy arrangement, but one that the purist may want to preserve.

Since the bore is cylindrical except for a slight constriction at the bottom, the clarinet is one of the easiest instruments to make, and the only peculiarity that might call for some special directions is the channel at the tip of the mouthpiece. The boring of the mouthpiece joint is carried out to the distance where the outside beak starts its sharp taper. Turning of the outside is completed, the flat is filed on the top, and the square wind channel then chiseled in to meet the bore. The beak is finally shaped with a spokeshave or a file to suit the player's preference. The flat does not extend right to the tip, for if it did there would be no space under the reed for passage of air. Therefore a curve is filed starting about 1 cm. from the tip at a radius such that there is a gap of about 1 mm. between the end of the reed and the end of the mouthpiece. There is a slight constriction in the bore of the lowest joint. This is produced by boring to $\frac{7}{16}$ in. and then using a tapered reamer.

Tuning is straightforward except for the peculiarity of the clarinet that makes it overblow a twelfth rather than an octave so that the lowest note in the low register is f, but in the high register it is c′. The gap between the two registers is filled (but incompletely) by use of the two keys. Opening either one of the keys gives a′, and opening both keys gives b′. If a player prefers, one of the two keyed holes (probably the top one) can be made

FIGURE 13. Clarinet.

slightly smaller so that opening both will give b-flat′, but there is no reliable way of providing both b′ and b-flat′ on this instrument. One of the two keys is also used to provide a vent for playing in the upper register. This key should have the smaller of the two holes, and the edges of the hole should be considerably rounded over.

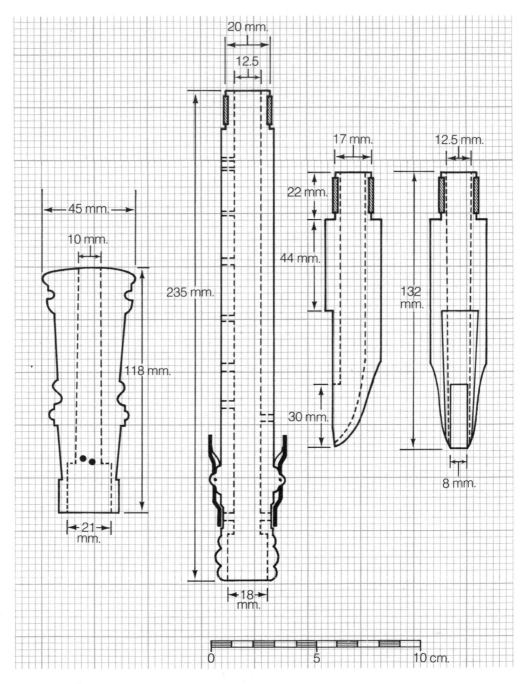

FIGURE 14. Clarinet.

TABLE 5.1
Clarinet Finger Hole Dimensions

Distances to centers of holes from top end.

Hole Number	Distance (mm.)	Diameter (mm.)
Keys 1 and 2	140	3.5
Thumb	185	5.0
1	192	3.5
2	210	4.5
3A	232	3.0
3B	236	3.0
4A	261	2.5
4B	261	2.5
5	285	3.0
6A	306	2.5
6B	310	1.5
7A	348	2.0
7B	350	2.5

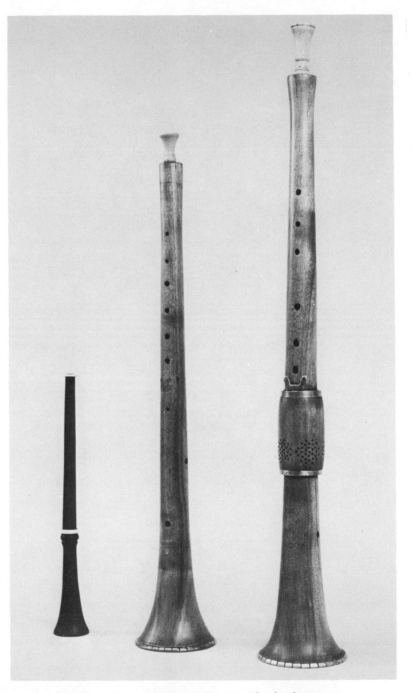

FIGURE 15. *Left*, musette; *center*, soprano shawm; *right*, alto shawm.

6
Shawm and Oboe

The origin of double-reed instruments, like most others, is vague and lost to us; but it is generally accepted that the lineage of the modern oboe reaches back to medieval times when shawms were introduced into Europe from the Near East. The shawm had a rather wide conical bore and used a large reed that gave a loud, coarse sound. Most shawms were also fitted with a device called a *pirouette* that enclosed the bottom end of the reed. The player's lips were pressed against this, and the tip of the reed was in his mouth. Therefore the vibration of the reed could not be controlled by the pressure of the lips, and overblowing was difficult. The shawms were essential members of wind bands in the fifteenth and sixteenth centuries. During the seventeenth century they were gradually refined with narrowing of the bore, elimination of the pirouette, and reduction of the size of the reed. Instruments of this transition period are distinguished from the earlier shawms by the name *Deutsche Schalmei*. They are more commonly seen in museum collections than are the earlier shawms, and some modern reproductions purporting to be shawms are, in fact, examples of the Deutsche Schalmei. The soprano Deutsche Schalmei can be readily recognized by its peculiarity of having a fontanelle that covers only a tuning hole, not a key mechanism (an example is no. 129 in the Boston Museum of Fine Arts collection). In the first half of the eighteenth century the shawm was already regarded as an obsolete instrument, and a recognizable oboe had emerged that then remained essentially unchanged until the early nineteenth century when further narrowing of the bore and the addition of keys began to lead towards the instrument of today.

In addition to a standard soprano shawm, I am giving dimensions (table 6.1) for a shawm pitched differently from any in the recognized shawm family, one that is considered to be a type of folk instrument rather than one used by professional musicians. The two highest pitched shawms described by Praetorius went down to b′ and e′, and the low note of the one described here is f′. This gives it the more common F fingering so that it can be played more readily. Folk instruments of this type are sometimes called pastoral pipes or musettes, although the name musette

FIGURE 16. *Left*, oboe d'amore; *center*, oboe in baroque pitch; *right*, oboe in modern pitch.

more often refers to a type of bagpipe that was popular among the aristocrats of seventeenth-century France. Indeed the chanter pipe of the bagpipe is not much different from this simple musette, and this similarity presumably accounts for the correspondence in name.

The bore of all of these instruments is narrower at the upper end than the smallest ($\frac{1}{4}$ in.) Ridgway shell auger. Therefore the boring cannot be carried straight through. It is necessary to stop short of the end and to finish with a twist drill.

A word also needs to be said about the bell, since shawms and oboes are the only wooden instruments described in this book that do have a flared bell. To turn the inside of this bell it is necessary to support the turning with a steady rest near the open end while driving the work with a chuck. Therefore the outside must be turned round after boring the bell joint but before reaming the inside to its final dimensions. A spear-pointed chisel suffices for shaping the shawm bells, but an L-shaped chisel is required for shaping the undercut lip on the oboe. One can be ground from an old file or made from an offset screwdriver by making the hoe-shaped end into a tang and sharpening the other end. It will be noticed (figs. 19, 20) that on the oboe there is a slight step in the bore where the middle joint meets the bell joint. This abrupt expansion of the bore is an essential characteristic of old oboes, and in some specimens the diameter increase is as much as 5 mm.

Reeds are a problem in the reproduction of old instruments, since so few original reeds have survived to our time. The musette does very well with a modern oboe reed. There is considerable difference of opinion about the proper reed dimensions for a baroque oboe (although "considerable" in this case refers to a millimeter more or less). The oboes here are in pitch if played with a modern oboe reed placed on a staple longer than usual or with a reed of about the dimensions of an English horn reed. If one is not appalled at such a liberty, a bagpipe practice chanter reed shortened to about 22 mm. will also work, but the tone will be harsher than it should properly be. In the soprano shawm a brass staple such as a modern oboe staple fits into the end of the instrument, the pirouette is pushed onto it, and a reed is then fitted to the staple. A bagpipe reed can be used if the player does not wish to experiment with making his own.

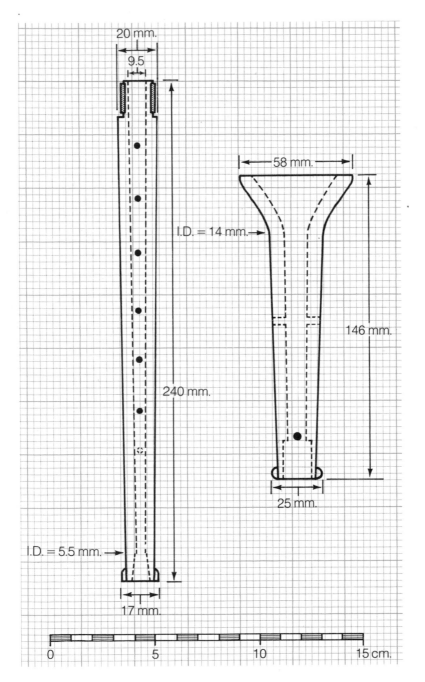

FIGURE 17. A copy of a musette in the Boston Museum of Fine Arts collection (no. 127). The original is made of rosewood with ivory rings.

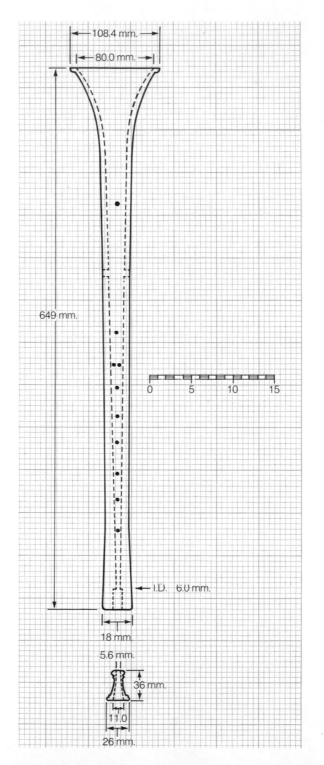

FIGURE 18. Soprano shawm. A composite of two original instruments in the Brussels collection (nos. 2,323 and 2,324).

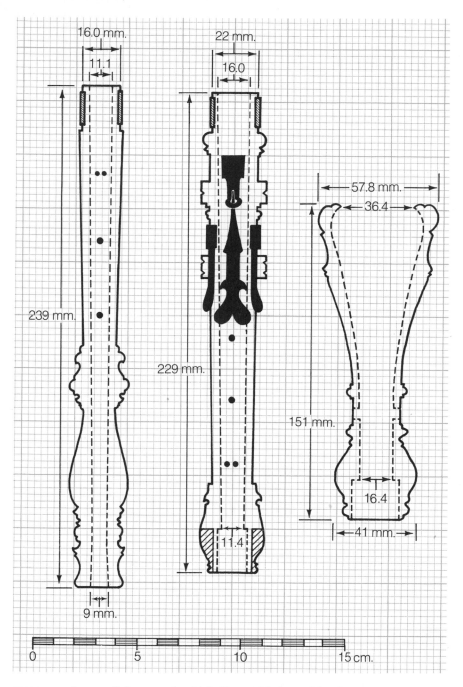

16.0 mm.

11.1

22 mm.

16.0

57.8 mm.

36.4

239 mm.

229 mm.

151 mm.

16.4

11.4

41 mm.

9 mm.

0   5   10   15 cm.

FIGURE 19. A copy of a baroque oboe in the Boston Museum of Fine Arts
collection (no. 133). The original is made of pearwood.

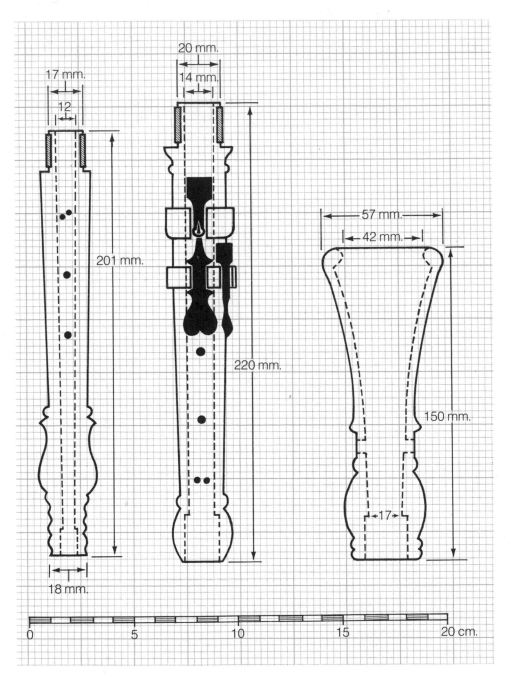

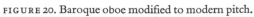

FIGURE 20. Baroque oboe modified to modern pitch.

TABLE 6.1

Shawm Hole Dimensions

Distances measured from top end to centers of holes.

Hole Number	Soprano Shawm		Musette	
	Distance (mm.)	Diameter (mm.)	Distance (mm.)	Diameter (mm.)
Thumb	—	—	60	3.5
I	95	5.0	80	3.0
2	132	5.0	105	4.0
3	162	6.9	128	4.0
4	199	6.7	157	3.5
5	233	7.0	183	3.5
6	267	7.0	208	3.5
7	293*	4.0	241	4.0
8	332	5.0	—	—
Tuning Holes	403	8.0	299	3.5
	485†	8.0	—	—

* The left-hand hole is plugged.
† Holes in top and bottom.

TABLE 6.2

Oboe Hole Dimensions

Distances are measured from top end to centers of holes.

Hole Number	Original		Modern Pitch	
	Distance (mm.)	Diameter (mm.)	Distance (mm.)	Diameter (mm.)
1	130	3.0	108	3.0
2	166	3.0	137	3.0
3A	197	2.0	162	2.0
3B	197	2.0	167	2.0
4A	259	3.6	224	2.5
4B	259	3.6	227	2.5
5	290	4.7	254	4.0
6	319	4.6	285	4.5
7	365	6.0	335	4.5
8	403	8.3	363	6.0
Tuning Holes	471	5.4	438	7.0

7
Krumhorns

Krumhorns (Cromornes) came into use in Europe at the end of the fifteenth century and were perhaps derived from folk instruments of the period. The krumhorn consort was a favorite ensemble during the sixteenth century and lasted until the end of the seventeenth century. As a soft, reed instrument the krumhorn has much to recommend it. It blends well with recorders, providing a low-pitched instrument with a stronger sound than the low-pitched recorders. It is rather easy to play, and its fingering is the same as recorder fingering. Its chief disadvantage is the limited range. Since the reed is enclosed (fig. 22) and cannot be squeezed with the lips, the overblowing capacity is severely limited. A range of only a ninth can be expected, although it may be possible to overblow the soprano krumhorn as high as f″; and modern reproductions of krumhorns sometimes have added keys to increase the range upward by two or three notes. Although such keys were not used on the classical krumhorns, similar keys were sometimes present on other instruments of the time.

Seven sizes of krumhorns have been described ranging from the extended great bass, whose lowest note is F′, to the descant (soprano), whose lowest note is c′. The most commonly recognized four sizes, soprano, alto, tenor, and bass, cover the range from F to d″, that is, each one is pitched an octave below the correspondingly named instrument of the recorder family.

The obvious peculiarity in construction of the krumhorn is the bending of the tube. The first steps are, as in other wooden instruments, boring with the $\frac{1}{4}$-in. diameter shell auger and turning the outside diameter. Then the wood is steamed and bent. Certain kinds of wood are most amenable to steam bending although several species have been used. Renaissance krumhorns were often made of boxwood and may have been made by drilling out the pith from young, green trunks of the plant, bending them, and allowing them to season in the bent form. This is not a very practical procedure for the present-day worker. I have been successful in making krumhorns of maple, cherry, and magnolia, but by far the best wood for this purpose seems to be black walnut. Some modern reproductions are made of Brazilian rosewood. Before the actual steaming it is helpful to soak the piece of wood in water

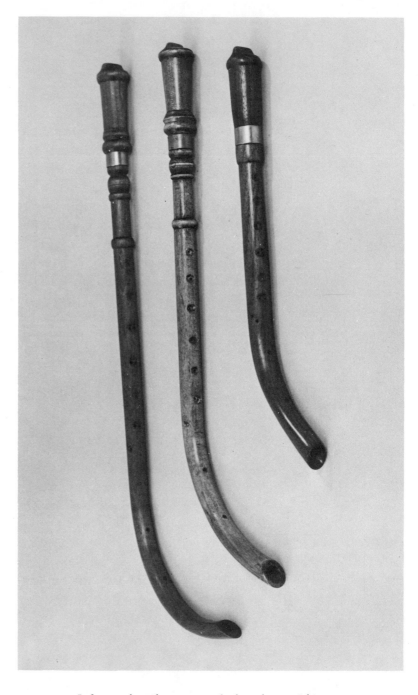

FIGURE 21. *Left*, tenor krumhorn; *center*, alto krumhorn; *right*, soprano krumhorn.

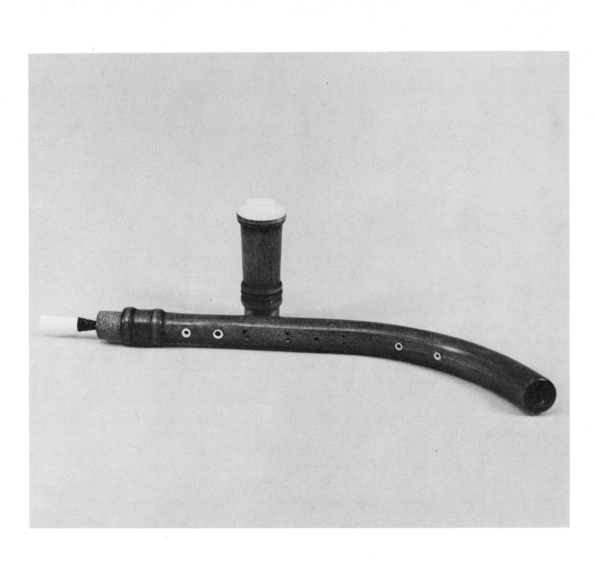

FIGURE 22. Soprano krumhorn with cap removed.

overnight. A simple steaming chamber can be put together from
a teakettle, a length of hose, and a piece of 3-in. or 4-in. diameter
sheet metal pipe arranged so that condensed water runs back into
the kettle. A metal strap to support the outside of the curve must
be prepared, and for this purpose a length of pipe-hanging strap
can be used with wooden blocks fastened to it at a distance apart
exactly equal to the length of the piece to be bent. It is a good idea
to allow about $\frac{1}{2}$ in. to 1 in. extra at each end of the wood, since
the ends may be damaged during the bending. After steaming
for about three hours, the piece is placed into the metal strap,
bent over a form of suitable radius, and clamped in place to dry
for forty-eight hours. Separation of the wood fibers during bending can be minimized if the bend is made so that the growth
rings in the wood are parallel to the plane of the curve. A 4-in.
radius gives a satisfactory shape for all sizes of krumhorns and is
not too sharp to be readily made. Figure 23 illustrates the metal
strap and one form of bending jig.

After boring and turning the cap, the air channel is made by drilling a row of holes and filing away the waste wood between them.
The beak shape is then cut with a coping saw, and the brass
ferrule is fitted.

The simplest way to provide reeds for the soprano and alto
krumhorns is to buy bagpipe practice chanter reeds, which cost
between fifty cents and a dollar apiece. The only modification
that may be necessary is to scrape the tip a little thinner. If the
sound is too rattly this can be improved by wrapping a ligature
of thin brass wire around the reed and sliding it up and down to
find the best position. For the tenor krumhorn a larger reed is
required and can be made as follows. A mandrel is turned with
a taper from 6.5 mm. to 2 mm. over a length of 50 mm. Thin
copper or brass is cut following a paper template then bent and
hammered around the mandrel to make a staple for the reed.
The seam can be soldered, but this is probably not necessary.
The small end is flattened into an elliptical cross-section. The two
leaves of the reed are cut from a plastic sheet about 0.01 in. to
0.0125 in. thick in the shape shown in figure 25. Soft vinyl such
as is used for many throwaway articles is quite suitable for low-

FIGURE 23. Bending jig and supporting strap for krumhorns.

pitched instruments, but if reeds are to be made for soprano and alto krumhorns, a stiffer, crisper type of plastic must be used. The two leaves are clamped together in a spring clamp so that the tapered end and about 1 cm. of the straight-sided portion stick out. With strong thread tie a clove hitch around the notches in the reed, leaving about a 2-in. end on the thread. Coat the staple with some fast-drying cement and insert it between the leaves of the reed so that its tip does not quite reach to the straight-sided part of the reed. Then wrap the thread tightly around the reed so that the edges are pulled together over the mandrel. The wrapping should extend from just above the notch down to the tip of the plastic. It is finished off by tying a square knot to the loose end that was left at the beginning. The reed should now be removed from the clamp and bent into a flattened ellipse open at the tip. The parallel sides must touch all along their length. If there is a gap just above the wrapping, it means that the wrapping is not tight enough or that the staple extends too far into the reed. The lower part of the staple is next wrapped with lapping thread started and finished in the same way as the other but with enough layers to make a tight fit in the socket of the instrument. Fast-drying cement or shellac spread over the upper wrapping and the ends of the lapping thread fixes it in place and seals any small air leaks. When the coating has dried, the reed is finished by scraping it with a sharp knife or a razor blade. The tip needs to be very thin, and the rest of the reed is scraped and tested in the instrument until a clear note can be played. Before any tone holes are made in the tenor krumhorn, this note will be in the vicinity of G. Too thick a reed will overblow to a much higher note if it sounds at all.

The tuning of the krumhorn is peculiar in that usually two (but sometimes one or three) tuning holes are made below the lowest finger hole, and the lowest tone is controlled by these holes rather than by the total length of the instrument. Another peculiarity is that the pitch of any note can be varied through at least a full tone by varying the blowing pressure. Therefore in tuning, the diameter of each finger hole should be made to give the right note with an intermediate blowing pressure; then if occasion

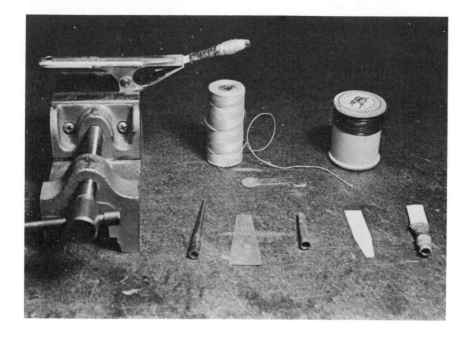

FIGURE 24. Reed making tools and supplies: *left*, reed in clamp; *upper right*, thread; *center*, key pattern; *lower right, from left to right*, mandrel; staple blank; finished staple; leaf of reed; finished reed.

demands the pitch can be either raised or lowered by changing the pressure. Removing the fuzz from the inside of the tone holes is especially difficult with the krumhorn because of the bend and because the holes are so small. It must be removed, however, to get a clear tone. One procedure that works fairly well is to take a piece of stranded wire cable such as is used for bicycle caliper brakes, unlay several strands in the middle of the length, and insert a tuft of coarse steel wool. By pulling the cable back and forth through the bore, small splinters of wood can be pulled off from the underside of the tone holes.

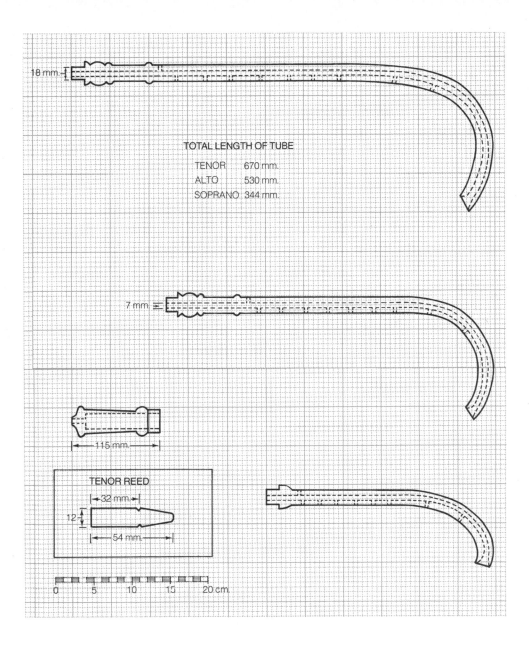

18 mm.

TOTAL LENGTH OF TUBE

TENOR	670 mm.
ALTO	530 mm.
SOPRANO	344 mm.

7 mm.

115 mm.

TENOR REED

32 mm.

12

54 mm.

0   5   10   15   20 cm.

FIGURE 25. Three krumhorns. The same size wind cap is used for all three.

TABLE 7.1

Krumhorn Hole Dimensions

Distances are measured from top end of main tube to centers of holes.

Hole Number	Soprano Distance (mm.)	Diameter (mm.)	Alto Distance (mm.)	Diameter (mm.)	Tenor Distance (mm.)	Diameter (mm.)
Thumb	42	4.0	108	3.0	127	3.0
1	48	3.5	122	3.5	130	2.5
2	70	3.0	150	3.0	167	3.5
3	94	3.0	180	3.5	203	4.0
4	120	3.0	212	2.5	240	4.0
5	144	2.0	245	3.0	278	2.5
6A	162	2.0	271	2.5	310	2.5
6B	165	2.0	273	2.5	312	2.5
7A	176	2.0	297	1.5	330	2.0
7B	182	2.0	300	1.5	335	2.0
Tuning A	214	4.0	344	2.5	425	3.5
Tuning B	263	4.0	398	2.5	484	3.5

8
Racketts

The racketts or sausage bassoons were a family of instruments introduced late in the sixteenth century and already superseded by bassoons at the end of the seventeenth century. The concept of achieving a long-bored, bass instrument by interconnecting several short tubes within a single block of wood is theoretically sound, and being able to carry in one's pocket an instrument that will descend as low in pitch as a modern bassoon is still a very attractive idea. What doomed the rackett was probably not so much its quiet sound that blends well with recorders and krumhorns but rather its intractable fingering pattern. Some racketts had as many as sixteen holes to be controlled so that some holes were covered by the palms of the hands and the middle joints of the fingers. The sequence of uncovering holes to produce a scale appears from the outside of the instrument to follow a random pattern and, worse, is not the same from member to member of the rackett family. The family as described by Praetorius consisted of four sizes: cant, tenor-alto, bass, and great bass. The two instruments for which dimensions are given here (table 8.1) correspond roughly to the cant and tenor-alto, although in the interests of simplicity the number of finger holes has been reduced so that their ranges are not so wide as those in the racketts described by Praetorius. The cant covers the range from F to g and the tenor-alto from C to e, while Praetorius' instruments had a range of a twelfth.

Since the bores are all cylindrical and relatively short, they can be made with the drill press by laying out the work carefully and drilling from both ends; or the boring can be done in the lathe with a shell auger if a four-jaw chuck is used so that the piece can be set off-center to drill the six outside holes. When the bores have been made, the outside is turned down to be concentric with the center bore, and the interconnecting passages are chiseled away between the bores. The end caps are turned so that the bottom one fits tightly and the top one is easily removable. Before gluing on the bottom end cap, I like to glue a piece of stiff paper or cambric to the bottom with contact cement to make sure that no leaks between neighboring bores exist where they should not. The arrangement I have devised for fastening the top cap is, of

FIGURE 26. A family of racketts.

course, not traditional, but it is important to have the top cap easily removable to permit evaporation of moisture after playing, and it is also essential to avoid the slightest trace of air leakage between bores. Other arrangements that I have seen or tried fail to satisfy both of these requirements. The $\frac{1}{8}$-in. brass pipe nipple is fastened to the center bore by cutting a thread in the wood with an ordinary pipe tap. The nut that screws down on the cap must be made by drilling, knurling, and tapping a short length of brass rod. The pad of soft leather that fits into the cap should be well greased and will then make a tight seal when the nut is tightened.

The diamond-shaped arrangement for the four holes at the end of the bore was common but not universal in these instruments. In the diagrams (fig. 27) the finger holes are indicated where they enter the bore, but it is advisable to drill some of them at an angle to make them more easily reached.

The brass pipe nipple should be drilled out so that its bore is nearly that of the main bore and the top end should be reamed with a tapered reamer to give a better seat for the reed staple. The reed is made of plastic in the same way as described for krumhorns (chap. 7). For the smaller rackett a reed of the same size as that for the tenor krumhorn may be used. For the tenor-alto it could be slightly larger.

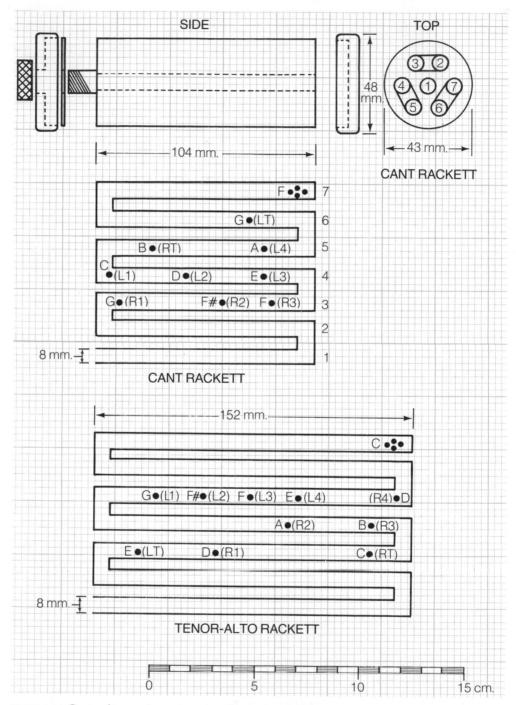

SIDE TOP

48 mm.

104 mm.

43 mm.

CANT RACKETT

F ●●●● 7
G ●(LT) 6
B ●(RT)   A ●(L4) 5
C
●(L1)   D ●(L2)   E ●(L3) 4
G●(R1)   F#●(R2) F ●(R3) 3
2
8 mm. 1

CANT RACKETT

152 mm.

C ●●●●

G●(L1) F#●(L2) F ●(L3) E ●(L4)   (R4)●D

A ●(R2)   B ●(R3)

E ●(LT)   D ●(R1)   C●(RT)

8 mm.

TENOR-ALTO RACKETT

0   5   10   15 cm.

FIGURE 27. Cant and tenor-alto racketts showing the finger positions.

TABLE 8.1
Rackett Hole Dimensions

See figure 27 for hole locations.

Cant		Tenor-Alto	
Hole Designation	Diameter (mm.)	Hole Designation	Diameter (mm.)
G	2.0	E	2.5
F-sharp	2.0	D	2.5
F	2.0	C	2.5
E	3.0	B	2.5
D	2.5	A	2.0
C	2.0	G	2.0
B	2.0	F-sharp	2.0
A	2.0	F	2.0
G	2.0	E	1.5
F (4 holes)	2.0	D	2.0
		C (5 holes)	2.0

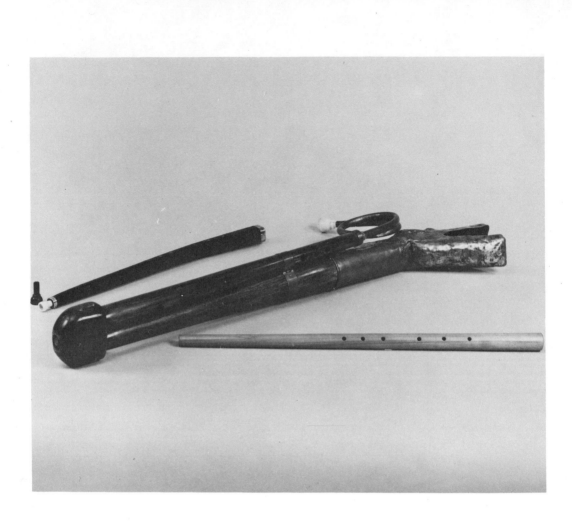

FIGURE 28. *Left*, curved cornett; *center*, Russian bassoon; *right*, mute cornett. The Russian bassoon may be considered a bass member of this family, although it dates from a later period.

9
Cornetti

The cornetto was an important instrument during the Middle Ages, Renaissance and the beginning of the baroque period. Actually there were three somewhat different instruments known by this name, and the terminology across three or four different languages becomes rather confusing. The curved instrument was the best known and the one that lasted the longest. It is and was known as a *cornett* (English), *krummer Zink* (German), *cornet recourbé* (French), or *cornetto curvo* (Italian). Since it was wrapped with black leather, it was also sometimes called a *black cornett*. It had a separate, cup-shaped mouthpiece made of ivory, horn, or wood. A straight version is known as *gerader Zink* (German), *cornet droit* (French), or *cornetto diritto* (Italian). It also had a separate mouthpiece, but it was not wrapped with leather. The third version was also straight, but its mouthpiece was turned as an integral part of the body and was more funnel shaped. It is known as a *mute cornett* (English), *stiller Zink* (German), or *cornetto muto* (Italian). All these names suggest its quieter sound. It was also known as a *white cornett* since it was not wrapped with black leather.

The dimensions given here for the curved cornetto result in an instrument in A. This is the traditional pitch of the most familiar size known as soprano. Both smaller and larger sizes existed. Because of the curved bore, this instrument must be made in two halves that are gouged out and then glued together with waterproof glue. Although leather was the traditional wrapping material, the instrument shown in figure 28 (*left*) was wrapped with black plastic tape, and the shine was dulled by rubbing with powdered pumice. If leather is used, the type known in the trade as *lamb skiver* is thin and flexible enough for the purpose. The finger holes should be made before wrapping, and the wrapping then carefully cut through at the holes. Since this instrument has an octagonal cross-section, the ferrules are made up of soldered strips rather than seamless tubing. The upper ferrule is especially important, since insertion of the mouthpiece tends to wedge apart the glue joint. Two sizes of mouthpiece are given. The smaller is more usual and facilitates playing in the upper range. The larger is less tiring and makes the lower range easier to play.

The boring and reaming of the mute cornett is straightforward except that the taper of $\frac{3}{8}$ in. per foot $(1:40)$ requires making special reamers; or like the curved cornett this one too can be glued up from two gouged-out halves, and the outside then turned. If it is bored from a solid piece, the boring must not be carried right through to the upper end, or the hole at the bottom of the mouthpiece cup will be too large. There is some latitude possible in the placement and the diameters of the finger holes of the mute cornett since lip adjustment allows a range of tones for any given finger position. The instrument whose dimensions are presented here is in the key of A. Its useful range begins at A_3 and extends upwards for about two octaves. By relaxing lip tension it is possible to play as much as an octave lower than the normal range, but the pitch of the notes so obtained is difficult to control, and the tone is unsatisfactory.

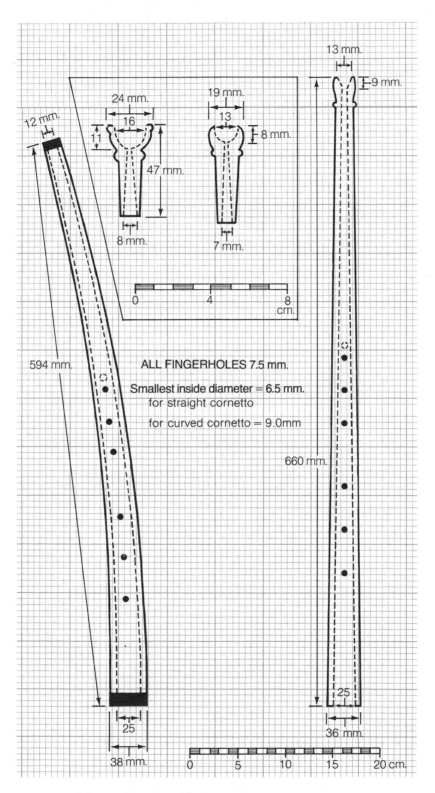

12 mm.

24 mm.
16
11
47 mm.
8 mm.

19 mm.
13
8 mm.
7 mm.

13 mm.
9 mm.

0   4   8
cm.

594 mm.

ALL FINGERHOLES 7.5 mm.

Smallest inside diameter = 6.5 mm.
for straight cornetto
for curved cornetto = 9.0mm

660 mm.

25
38 mm.

25
36 mm.

0   5   10   15   20 cm.

FIGURE 29. *Left*, curved cornett; *right*, mute cornett.

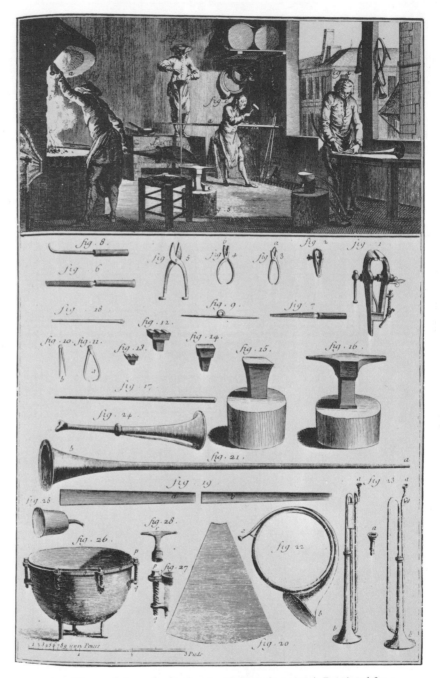

FIGURE 30. The workshop of a *chaudronnier* (eighteenth century). Reprinted from Diderot's *Encyclopédie*, volume 3, plate 4 of the volumes of plates (Paris, 1762–72).

10
Brass
Instruments
Materials and
Methods

In many respects reproductions of ancient brass instruments are easier to make than those of wooden instruments. For one thing, tuning is much simpler. Once the tube has been cut to the right length to give the proper fundamental note, all the other notes of the harmonic scale follow automatically. Since valves were not used on the old instruments, they were played at the high range of the harmonic series where available notes come closer together. For an instrument in the key of C the harmonic series is as follows:

C, c, g, c′, e′, g′, b-flat′, c″, d″, e″, f-sharp″, g″, a″, b-flat″, b″, c″′

The f-sharp″ and a″ of this series are noticeably flat, the f-sharp″ so much that by adjustment of the embouchure it can be used for f″, giving a complete major scale between c″ and c″′. Since b-flat″ is also available, the key of F can be played fairly well on old brass instruments in C. Instruments in D can be played fairly well in G, and instruments in F fairly well in B-flat. It is these limitations of the harmonic series that governed the choice of keys used by baroque and Renaissance composers for brass instrument compositions. Some tightly coiled clarino trumpets are now being made with two small finger holes to help in obtaining certain notes and correcting the pitch of the f-sharp″. Historical precedent for this construction is dubious.

The series of sixteen harmonics given above might not be all available on a single instrument, and on some instruments a skilled player might be able to reach still further to the twentieth or twenty-second harmonic. A narrow bore favors the higher harmonics but gives a weaker sound, while the converse is true of a wide bore. A shallow, cupped mouthpiece also makes it easier to attain the higher tones but again at a sacrifice of loudness.

Materials

With regard to materials, the typical brass instrument can be dissected into three portions: the cone and bell are shaped from thin sheet metal, the main cylindrical tube is purchased as a tube and only cut to size and bent by the instrument maker, and the mouthpiece is machined from a solid block of brass.

Although referred to generally as "brass" instruments, some old trumpets and horns were made of copper; and for the amateur instrument maker copper has much to recommend it. It is more readily available, less expensive, and easier to work. Copper sheet used for roofing is referred to in the trade as *16-oz. sheet*, meaning that a square foot weighs sixteen ounces. It measures 0.02 in. in thickness. Twenty-four- and thirty-two-oz. copper sheet is available from some sheet metal dealers. If it can be obtained, the 24-oz. sheet seems to be best for both the bell and the cone. The 16-oz. size is all right for the cone and is recommended for a cone that is to be curved, but it makes a bell that is lighter than it should be. The 32-oz. sheet is difficult to work, and the results obtained in most cases do not justify its expense. Brass is, of course, stiffer than copper and can therefore be used in thinner sheets. Brass shim stock of 0.020 in. is available in widths of 6 in. and 12 in. from dealers in industrial supplies, and it can be used for both bell and cone, although I generally prefer to use 0.032-in. brass for trumpet bells. Although less readily available, 0.025-in. brass makes a fine compromise for bell and cone.

For the tubing, copper again has advantages for the amateur in that copper water pipe is readily available from plumbing suppliers, and in the flexible L grade it is easily bent. Brass tubing can be found in a wider range of diameters than copper pipe, but dealers in it are much less common (see Appendix B).

Brass is the common material for turning mouthpieces, although some old mouthpieces were made of ivory, horn, or wood; and some modern mouthpieces are made of plastic (usually acrylic). Aluminum mouthpieces are unsatisfactory because they blacken the player's lips. It is a waste of brass to turn the whole mouthpiece from a rod the diameter of the widest part, since the shank of the mouthpiece is so much smaller. The best solution is to make rough castings larger than the finished mouthpiece but of a similar shape and then to finish them on the lathe. A small, gas-fired furnace (see Appendix B) will melt brass nicely, and either

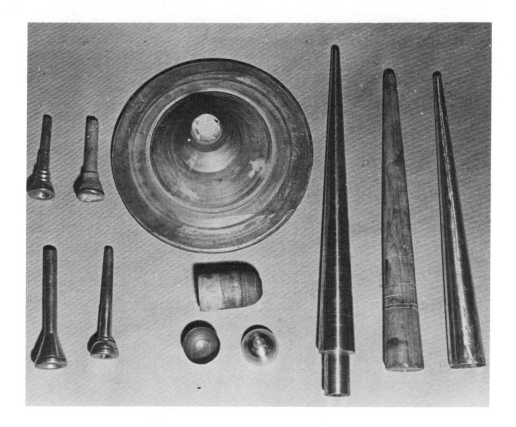

FIGURE 31. Brass instrument tools and parts: *left*, mouthpieces and a rough mouthpiece casting; *center*, forms for spinning bell and ball; *right*, steel and wooden mandrels and a seamed cone.

a sand mold or a permanent mold bored out of steel can be used. A simpler approach is to drill a hole through the center of a short length of large-diameter rod and solder a length of smaller diameter rod into it. When the mouthpiece is turned from this assembly, the solder joint will be inconspicuous.

General Construction

My approach to the general construction of brass instruments departs from tradition in that I make the bell and conical sections separately. As described in *The Making of Musical Instruments* by Young or illustrated in figure 32, these two parts were usually made of one piece of metal seamed along its length and then planished over a mandrel before spinning the bell to its final shape. This procedure is inconvenient for the amateur for several reasons, the chief one being that brazing is required. The approach I have adopted is used to some extent in industry today. For simplicity I have also decided to make the cylindrical part of the trumpet from only two pieces of tubing, whereas old trumpets normally used separate U-shaped pieces to join the ends of the straight tubes. The following very useful articles should be consulted for details on the construction of old trumpets: "William Bull and the English Baroque Trumpet," "Early British Trumpet Mouthpieces," and "Four Seventeenth Century British Trumpets," by E. Halfpenny; "Further Notes on the British Trumpets," by J. Wheeler; and "The Trumpets of J. W. Haas," by D. Smithers.

Spinning the Bell

For basic information on the technique of metal spinning, the beginner should consult one of a number of instruction books dealing with lathe operation or metalworking. As a word of encouragement, though, it may be remarked that trumpet and

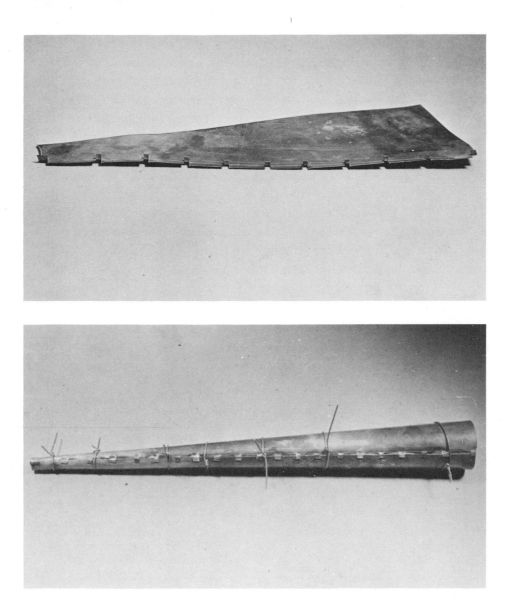

FIGURE 32. Steps in forming and seaming a cone.

horn bells are relatively easy as metal spinning projects go. A wooden chuck must first be made from a fine-grained hardwood such as maple (see fig. 31) and soaped or waxed with beeswax. Both copper and brass bells require frequent annealing during the spinning process by heating them red hot and quenching them in cold water. I like to work on two bells at the same time so that one can be heating while I spin the other. It is a good idea to make a small scratch on the metal to line up with a mark on the chuck, because if the chuck is just slightly unsymmetrical, wrinkles will appear in the metal if it is put back with a different orientation. When the bell has been spun to its full size the edge is trued up with the diamond tool and rolled over with the beading tool. Before the bead is closed the rim can be strengthened by inserting a circle of copper wire into it. If this is done the wire must be prevented from rattling by running in solder or epoxy cement.

Forming the Cone

A seamless cone can be formed by spinning, either by starting with a disc and gradually spinning it down over a series of successively smaller diameter mandrels or by starting with a cylindrical tube which has a diameter equal to that of the large end of the finished cone and spinning it down around a conical mandrel. However, a seamed cone seems best for the amateur to make.

The simplest seamed cone is shaped around a wooden mandrel turned to the correct taper. The metal can be cut to size by wrapping brown paper tightly around the mandrel, gluing or taping it together, then cutting it square at top and bottom and slitting down its length. The paper pattern can then be traced on the metal adding about 5 mm. of width along one edge for the overlapping seam. A neater seam can be made if a narrow step is made along the mandrel so that one edge of the metal can be set against it. Both copper and brass should be thoroughly annealed before bending them around the mandrel. To hold the metal in place for soldering the seam, a series of steel rings is forced around it so that they are about 2 in. apart. Before forming the cone the surfaces to be soldered together should have been well cleaned and fluxed. Finally, with the heat from a torch, solder is run into the seam. For greater strength silver solder can be used, but even on cones that are to be curved later a good, soft soldered joint will hold. Finally, when the solder has hardened, the joint must be filed, ground, and buffed.

A stronger and smoother seam can be made by workers who can braze it with an oxygen torch. For this work a steel mandrel is required. The metal is cut to size just as before. Then a series of square notches is cut along one edge and the teeth raised. When the cone is formed around the mandrel the other edge butts against the raised teeth, which are hammered down over it to hold it in place (fig. 32). The seam is now brazed, washed to remove excess flux, and hammered down smoothly against the mandrel. Since the cone made in this way is essentially a homogeneous piece of metal, final smoothing of the seam can be done by putting the cone on its mandrel in the lathe and applying the flat spinning tool to it, then polishing it with abrasive cloth and buffing. The large end of the cone is finally hammered out into a smooth flare to meet the curve on the small end of the bell.

The Cylindrical Tube

For a straight herald's trumpet the only thing that must be done to the cylindrical tube is to enlarge one end into a short flare into which the conical portion will fit to a depth of an inch or so. This is done by heating the end of the tube red hot and driving in a steel mandrel which has the correct taper.

Most brass (or copper) instruments require bending of the tubing to achieve their final form. If brass is used, it must be well annealed even for bends of large diameter. Flexible copper water pipe does not require annealing.

Bends of large diameter, such as those in hunting horns, can be made easily with no danger of the tubing becoming flattened. For tight bends, however, it is necessary to fill the tubing with some material that will prevent collapse of the walls during the bending and can be readily removed later. Low melting alloys such as Wood's metal are used industrially for this purpose, but they are expensive. Pitch was one material used classically, and it is available quite cheaply from some suppliers of industrial chemicals or from tanners, since it is used for dehairing hides. The tubing is filled with melted pitch and, when the pitch has hardened, bent around a wooden form cut to the correct radius. The tube is then reheated so that the pitch melts and runs out. Thorough heating is required to insure complete removal of the pitch.

Assembly of the Parts

When the three sections described above have been made it is a simple matter to solder them together. The bell should fit into the cone about $\frac{1}{4}$ in. to $\frac{3}{8}$ in. and the cone into the tube about 1 in. The instrument is assembled with the bell pointing up, a weight put on to hold the joints tightly together, and solder run in with heat from a torch. If a soldered cone is used, the upper end must be tightly wrapped with steel wire to prevent it from spreading open when the solder melts. I think it is better to use soft solder for this assembly even if facilities for brazing are available, because disassembly for any later corrections is much simpler.

The Mouthpiece

The first principle of making a mouthpiece is the same as that for turning wooden instruments, that is, the bore is made first and the outside then turned to be concentric with it. A piece of brass, preferably shaped roughly as described earlier, is drilled

straight through its center with a drill equal in diameter to the
smallest part of the finished bore. The contour of the cup can be
shaped roughly using larger drills but not given its final form
until the last operation. A conical back bore can be reamed all the
way, but it is faster to make it by using increasingly larger drills
to give a series of steps that are then smoothed out with a tapered
reamer. After this boring has been done, the exterior of the
mouthpiece is turned between centers in the lathe. Finally the
cup is given its final shape by chucking the shank either in the
drill press or lathe and working on the cup with a rotary file held
in a suitable handle. Polishing is completed with rubber-bonded
abrasive wheels in the high-speed hand grinder and a buffing
wheel loaded with Tripoli compound.

Finishing

It is a good idea to polish individual parts to some extent before
final assembly, since it may be easier to get at them separately;
but an overall polishing operation will surely be needed at the
end, and it is a matter of working down from files through successively finer grades of abrasive cloth, rubber-bonded abrasive
wheels, and finally buffing on a cloth wheel with Tripoli compound. After that an occasional polishing with brass polish will
keep the instrument shiny. For those who wish to avoid the
polishing chore, a brass lacquer is available from instrument shops.

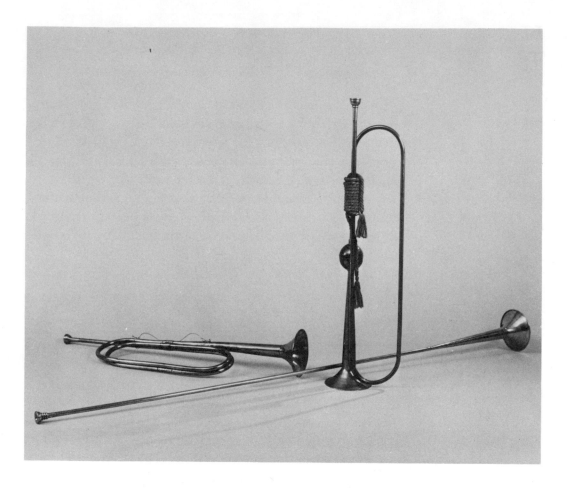

FIGURE 33. Some trumpets.

11
Trumpets

The trumpet is an instrument of great antiquity and widespread occurrence in one form or another. The special type that is considered here had its beginnings in Europe in the thirteenth and fourteenth centuries where it took the form of a flattened *S*. By the sixteenth century the twice-folded form of the tube had been standardized and remained mostly unchanged until the end of the eighteenth century. This twice-folded form is the design presented here in figure 34. The three parallel tubes are commonly designated *mouthpipe*, *middle pipe*, and *bell pipe*. Aside from the peculiarities of the mouthpiece (to be dealt with later), two things should be pointed out. The mouthpipe and bell pipe were usually not soldered together rigidly but held together only by the wooden block and wrapping towards the back end. Some believe that the tone is improved by this lack of rigidity. The ball in the middle of the bell pipe is also a standard feature of old trumpets. In the instrument shown in figures 33 and 34, as in some historical ones, it serves to cover a joint. It also serves as a handle for pressing the instrument firmly against the lips.

The construction procedure follows mostly without any special problems from the general methods discussed in chapter 10. There are several possible ways of fastening together the two J-shaped cylindrical sections. One can be flared slightly and the other fitted into it for soldering. A joint made in this way is weak by itself, and a reinforcing garnish should be soldered over the joint. If there is to be an extra garnish at this joint, the flaring might as well be dispensed with and a closely fitting section of tubing soldered over the joint.

The ball is spun as two hemispheres with a short, flaring skirt on one half into which the other half fits snugly (see fig. 31). Before soldering the halves together the holes for passage of the tubing should be drilled at the ends, starting the drill on the inside. Notice that the hole towards the bell must be larger than the hole towards the mouthpiece, but its final diameter can be adjusted with a reamer after the ball has been soldered together. Attachment of the ball to the tubing must be done by sliding the ball and the two reinforcing washers onto the cylindrical tube, flaring the end to receive the conical tube, soldering the two tubes together, and finally sliding the ball over the joint and soldering it in place. The other joints at the bell and in the middle pipe can be soldered at any time. The piece of wood between the bell and mouthpiece pipes is grooved along the edges with a gouge or router. The cord is wrapped around it following the same pattern illustrated in figure 4 for wrapping thread around the joints of woodwind instruments.

The dimensions given in figure 34 are for a trumpet in D, the most common of the baroque period. For a C trumpet it is necessary merely to increase the length of the cylindrical tubing by 1 ft., that is, by adding 4 in. to each of the three parallel sections of tubing. Small adjustments in pitch can be achieved by preparing a number of short lengths of tubing (called *bits*) that can be fitted between the mouthpiece and the mouthpiece pipe and held in place by a ferrule soldered either to the bit or to the end of the mouthpiece pipe. A loop of tubing can also be made for insertion here to lower the D trumpet to C; but since the diameter of such a loop is only about 3 in., it must be made of quite thin-walled tubing.

Three ranges of trumpet parts have been distinguished to take note of the differences between players and instruments so that if a composition was required to cover the full range of harmonics in the key of C, three instruments and three players might be required as follows:

> Principal e′–e″
> Clarino I g′–g″
> Clarino II c″–c″ ′ or higher

Most authors agree that the mouthpiece was of crucial importance in the design of the old trumpets, but they disagree on what its essential characteristics were. The most general agreement that can be reached is that the shape of the cup was a flattened hemisphere, not chamfered at the rim or at the grain, and that the rim was rather broad and flat. The volume of the cup, the diameter of the grain, and the shape of the back bore were apparently not standardized by any means. Cup diameters measured by Halfpenny as recorded in his articles, "William Bull and the English Baroque Trumpet," and "Early British Trumpet Mouthpieces," for a dozen old mouthpieces ranged from 16 mm. to 21 mm. and depths from 8.5 mm. to 13.2 mm. H. Eichborn, in *Die Trompete*, stresses the requirement for a narrow back bore for clarino playing, but grain diameters measured by Halfpenny ranged from 4 mm. to 7 mm.; and that for a modern mouthpiece falls within this range. The taper of the back bore was also quite variable. Some instruments measured by Halfpenny carried the grain diameter in a cylindrical section for about 20 mm. before starting to expand into a cone. Others had the shank formed of sheet metal and therefore no conical back bore at all. In *Encyclopaedia Britannica* (11th ed., s.v. "Trumpet") V. Mahillon describes a mouthpiece in which the grain diameter was carried through in a cylindrical bore for 10 cm., ending abruptly at the main bore; and he found that with such a mouthpiece extra notes could be obtained—indeed a continuous glissando from c to e″ could be played. Mahillon regards a mouthpiece of this type as probably a secret of the trumpeters' guilds, allowing initiates to play seemingly impossible passages. From his consideration of the subject Halfpenny arrived at the simple conclusion that "anyone determined enough could learn to blow any note with any mouthpiece" (*Galpin Society Journal*, p. 78), but he agrees with Eichborn that the fullness of tone is directly related to the volume of the cup (*Die Trompete*, p. 30).

J. E. Altenburg, one of the last of the great clarino players, wrote an excellent book on the trumpet in which he discusses the mouthpiece at some length, but sadly he does not give any precise measurements. The drawing he presents of the end view of his favorite mouthpiece cannot be interpreted as if it were an engineering drawing, but it does conform to the general characteristics of a broad rim and shallow cup. Some of Altenburg's general discussion from his book, *Versuch einer Einleitung zur heroisch-musikalischen Trompeter- und Pauker-Kunst*, seems well worth reproducing here in English translation.

> *. . .A rim that is too broad hinders the attack somewhat, since it takes away freedom of the lips and covers them too much. On the contrary a rim that is too narrow does not demand a precise and consistent attack and tires the lips in a short time.*

The so-called cup contributes much to the strength and weakness of the sound accordingly as it is deep or shallow, wide or narrow. One can strengthen the sound by a deep and wide cup which gives good service especially in field pieces and in the principal range. On the other hand a cup that is too shallow and narrow will not produce the required strength.

The interior opening brings forth, according to its narrowness or width, a corresponding height or depth of sound. If the air that is forced in is compressed in a small opening, it is able, because of its elasticity, to vibrate at the same time the resonant body and make it sound. On the other hand, if it spreads out into a wide opening and with little strength and pressure it will also bring forth only the low tones. . . .

Many provide themselves with a mouthpiece having a narrow cup and small hole with the intention of being able to reach the very high range. However, with this it is probably impossible to have a pure and bright tone in the high region as well as the low for heroic field pieces and the principal range. Therefore this kind of mouthpiece is not recommended to either the clarino or the principal player.

It is an especially important rule to accustom oneself only to a particular mouthpiece, because one can spoil his attack by frequent changes. Each must select a suitable mouthpiece according to the way his lips are formed and the range that he plays. That is, it would be out of place if a person with strong lips or [one] who plays the principal range were to choose a mouthpiece with a narrow cup and small opening. . . .
[pp. 81–82, my translation]

The design given here (fig. 35) is a kind of average based on Halfpenny's measurements and other descriptions. Following the general principles presented by Altenburg, it can be modified to suit particular needs.

For the final word here on trumpet mouthpiece design, Benade has suggested to me that a properly made mouthpiece will sound at about a″ (880Hz) when the rim is slapped on the palm of the hand. This pitch is controlled by cup volume, grain diameter and backbore and can therefore be adjusted by varying any one of these dimensions.

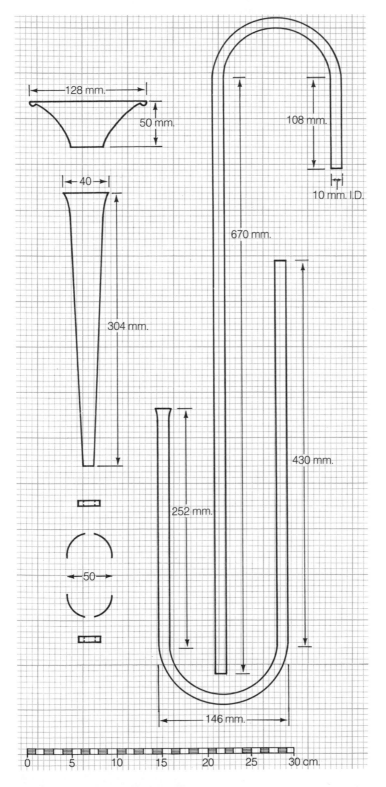

128 mm.

50 mm.

40

108 mm.

10 mm. I.D.

304 mm.

670 mm.

430 mm.

252 mm.

50

146 mm.

0   5   10   15   20   25   30 cm.

FIGURE 34. Trumpet in the key of D.

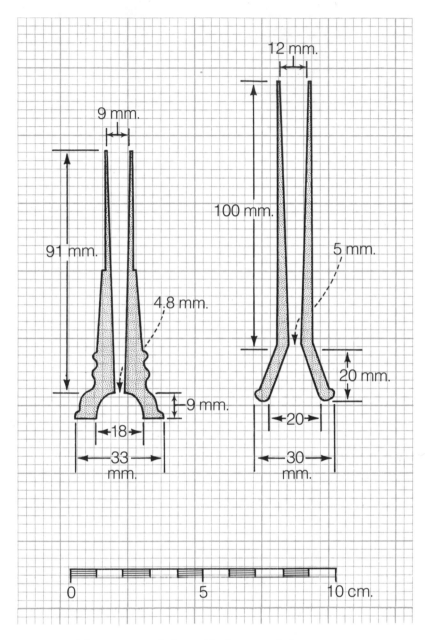

FIGURE 35. *left*, trumpet mouthpiece; *right*, horn mouthpiece.

12
Horns

The ancestry of today's horns can be traced back to instruments made of animal horns. The clearest distinction between the horn family and the trumpet family is that instruments of the former have a conical bore throughout their length, whereas the trumpets start flaring into a cone only near the open end. For at least the last two centuries there has also been a distinction in the shape of the mouthpiece: trumpets have a cup whose bottom makes a distinct angle with the start of the backbore, while horn mouthpieces have an elongated funnel shape blending rather unobtrusively into the backbore. The European hunting horn was first accepted into the orchestra in the eighteenth century and began its development towards the sophisticated French horn of today.

The simple hunting horn shown in figure 36 is nothing more than a conical tube 17 in. long with a small bell made as described in chapter 10. It has a shallow trumpet type of mouthpiece and can sound only two or three notes. The bend was made (after filling it with pitch) so that the soldered seam was along the concave side of the curve.

The larger hoop-shaped horn shown in figure 36 is not strictly speaking a true horn, since its bore is cylindrical for most of the length; but as a result of the form of the mouthpiece its tone is distinctly that of a horn. For a horn in F (the most usual key) the main tube consists of 11 ft. of $\frac{1}{2}$-in. copper tubing, the conical part is $15\frac{1}{2}$ in. long expanding to a diameter of $1\frac{1}{2}$ in., and the bell has a diameter of $7\frac{1}{2}$ in. The outside diameter of the loop is 18 in. The mouthpiece is made with a very long conical backbore. The dimensions given in figure 35 can be achieved by reaming the backbore with a so-called repairman's reamer obtainable in most hardware stores. In order to conserve brass and avoid making a special casting, the mouthpiece shown was made in two parts soldered together as described in chapter 10.

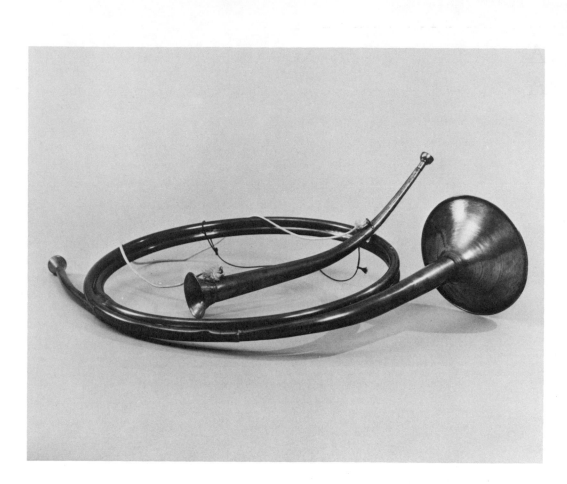

FIGURE 36. Horns.

Appendix A

Some Museum Collections of Instruments

Anyone who plans to visit any of the collections listed here should write ahead, since many of the museums are open to the public for only short periods and at unusual times.

Catalogs: ★ A catalog is available or in preparation; † A catalog has been published but is out of print.

AUSTRIA

Kunsthistorische Museum★
Neue Burg
Vienna

Museum Carolino Augusteum†
Salzburg, Postfach 525
Museumplatz 6

Oberösterreichischen Landesmuseum★
Linz

BELGIUM

Musée Instrumental†
Conservatoire Royal de Musique
17 Petit Sablon
Brussels

Vleeshuis Museum★
Antwerp

CZECHOSLOVAKIA

Národní Museum
Velkop řevorské náměští 4
Malá Strana
Prague I

DENMARK

Musikhistorisk Museet†
Aabenraa 32–34
1124 Copenhagen K

FRANCE

Musée du Conservatoire National de Musique†
rue de Madrid
Paris

GERMANY

Bavarian National Museum†
Munich

Deutsches Museum
Munich

Germanisches Museum
Untere Grasergasse 18
Nuremberg

Leipzig Musikinstrumenten-Museum★
Karl Marx Universität
Leipzig

Staatliches Institut für Musikforschung†
1 Berlin 15
Bundesallee 1–12

Stadtisches Museum†
Braunschweig

GREAT BRITAIN

Ashmolean Museum
Oxford

Donaldson Collection
Royal College of Music
London

The Galpin Society Collection
Reid School of Music
Park Place
Edinburgh 8

Horniman Museum†
London Road
Forest Hill
London s.e.23

Philip Bate Collection★
The Music Faculty
Oxford University
33 Holywell Street
Oxford

Pitt Rivers Museum★
Oxford

Ridley Collection
Luton Museum
Luton

Sheffield City Museum★
Sheffield

Victoria and Albert Museum★
Cromwell Road
London s.w.7

HUNGARY

Nemzeti Múzeum
Múzeum kit 14–16
Budapest

ITALY

Accademia Filharmonica
Via dei Mutilati 4/L
Verona

Biblioteca Capitolare★
Verona

Conservatorio Benedetto Marcello
Venice

Museo Civico
Bologna

Museo Civico★
Modena

Museo del Conservatorio Luigi Cherubini★
Florence

Museo Nazionale Scienza e Tecnica
Via S. Vittore 21
Milan

Museo Strumenti Musicali★
Castello Sforzesco
Milan

NETHERLANDS

Gemeente Museum★
Kon. Emma Kade
The Hague

POLAND

Museum of Musical Instruments
Old Market Square
Poznan

SOVIET UNION

Institute of Theater, Music, and Cinematography
Leningrad

SPAIN

Municipal Museum of Music
School of Music
110 Bruch Avenue
Barcelona

SWEDEN

Musikhistoriska Museet†
Slottsbacken 6
Stockholm

SWITZERLAND

Bernoulli Music Instrument Collection
Greifensee

Sammlung Alter Musikinstrumente†
Leonhardstrasse
Basel

UNITED STATES

Casadesus Collection†
Symphony Hall
Boston, Massachusetts 02115

The Dayton C. Miller Flute Collection★
The Library of Congress
Washington, D.C. 20540

Division of Musical Instruments★
National Museum of History and Technology
Smithsonian Institution
Washington, D.C. 20560

The Metropolitan Museum of Art†
5th Avenue and 82nd Street
New York, New York 10028

Museum of Fine Arts★
Huntington Avenue
Boston, Massachusetts 02115

Stearns Collection of Musical Instruments†
University of Michigan
Ann Arbor, Michigan 48104

Yale Collection of Musical Instruments★
Yale University
New Haven, Connecticut 06511

Appendix B

Sources of Materials

Albert Constantine and Son, Inc.
2050 Eastchester Road
Bronx, New York 10461

Craftsman Wood Service Co.
2727 South Mary Street
Chicago, Illinois 60608

General Woodwork Supplies
76–80 Stoke Newington High Street
London N.16
England

Joseph Gardner Hardwoods, Ltd.
Twig Folly Wharf
Roman Road
London E2 05J
England

Theodor Nagel Holzimport
2 Hamburg 28
Billstrasse 118
Germany

Wood Product Specialties
30 Bartholomew Avenue
Hartford, Connecticut 06106

The Woodshed
5 Avenue A
New York, New York 10009

TOOLS

Allcraft Tool and Supply Co.
215 Park Avenue
Hicksville, New York 11801
(*metal spinning tools and buffing supplies*)

Ash and Co.
5100 C Grand River
Detroit, Michigan 48208
(*machinists' tools and tapered reamers*)

Brookstone Company
Brookstone Building
Peterborough, New Hampshire 03458
(*fine small tools, files, and silver solder*)

Kitts Surplus Sales
Box 141, 21724 Albion
Farmington, Michigan 48024
(*machinists' tools, drills, and reamers*)

William Ridgway and Sons Ltd.
Oscar Works, Meadow Street
Sheffield s3 7BP
England
(*shell augers for long hole boring*)

Woodcraft Supply Corp.
313 Montvale Avenue
Woburn, Massachusetts 01801
(*fine woodworking tools, turning and carving chisels*)

METALS
(tubing, rods, and sheet)

Americraft Metals
Box B
Mohawk, New York 13407
(*also metalworking tools*)

Small Parts Inc.
6901 NE Third Avenue
Miami, Florida 33138
(*tubing in 1-ft. lengths only*)

FOUNDRY

Kansas City Specialties Co.
2805 Middleton Beach Road
Middleton, Wisconsin 53562
(*several sizes of small gas-fired
furnaces excellent for
brass casting or steel forging*)

IVORY
(Except where noted, pieces
can be ordered cut to
specified sizes.)

C. Dietrich
1 Berlin 15
Bundesallee 221
West Germany

F. Friedlein and Co., Ltd.
Kudu House
60 Minories
London E.C.3
England

H. Harris Ivory Works
St. Ives
Cornwall
England

E. Miltenberg, Inc.
300 Park Avenue South
New York, New York 10010
(*whole points only ; the smallest is about 4 lbs.*)

MUSICAL INSTRUMENT SUPPLIES

Erick Brand
1117 W. Beardsley Avenue
Elkhart, Indiana 46514
(*tools and repair supplies*)

Globe Musical Supply Co.
3522 Church Avenue
Brooklyn, New York 11203
(*reeds*)

Scottish Crafts
16 Newbury Street
Boston, Massachusetts
(*bagpipe reeds and hemp thread for joints*)

Appendix C

Making Shell Augers

A reasonable substitute for the commercial shell auger for boring long, straight holes can be made with some effort if it is too inconvenient to obtain the others. The stages of manufacture are sketched in figure 37. A length of drill rod $\frac{1}{16}$ in. to $\frac{1}{8}$ in. less in diameter than the diameter of the desired hole is used, heated red hot, and flattened on the anvil for a distance of $3\frac{1}{2}$ in. to 4 in. back from the end. The flattened section is again heated and hammered around an anvil of the proper radius. After this operation, the end view should show a half-circle section with the center of the arc in line with the center of the main piece of rod. A longitudinal slit is next made for a distance about equal to the diameter of the arc and dividing it in the ratio of $1:2$. The tip is again heated red hot and the two sections bent in almost to a right angle with the narrower piece overlapping the wider one. The overlapping edge will be the cutting edge of the bit, and it should be ground and sharpened so that its leading point is at the axis of the auger. Finally the tip should be reheated, quenched, and tempered.

A flat-tipped bit, which will not bore straight by itself but is useful for enlarging a hole made by one of the others, is made by starting the process as above. Then, when the end has been hammered flat, the tip is simply ground to a 60° V-shape with the cutting edges slightly relieved.

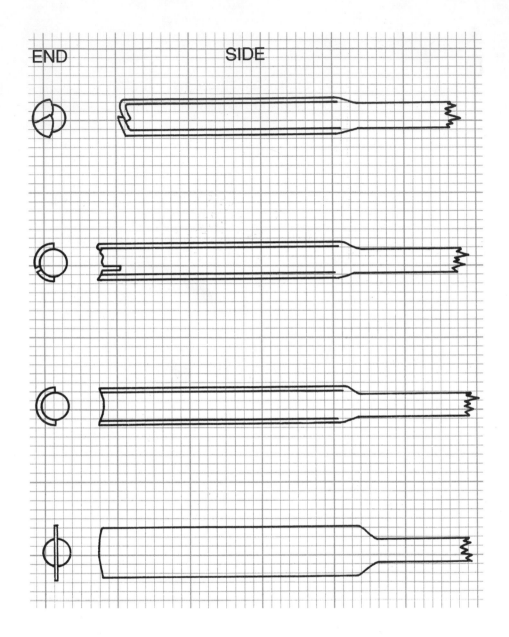

END   SIDE

FIGURE 37. Making a shell auger.

Appendix D

Table of Decimal Inches and Metric Equivalents

Inch	Decimal Inch	Millimeter	Inch	Decimal Inch	Millimeter
$\frac{1}{64}$	0.015625	0.396785	$\frac{17}{64}$	0.265625	6.746875
$\frac{1}{32}$	0.03125	0.79375	$\frac{9}{32}$	0.28125	7.14375
$\frac{3}{64}$	0.046875	1.190625	$\frac{19}{64}$	0.296875	7.540625
$\frac{1}{16}$	0.0625	1.5875	$\frac{5}{16}$	0.3125	7.9375
$\frac{5}{64}$	0.078125	1.984375	$\frac{21}{64}$	0.328125	8.334375
$\frac{3}{32}$	0.09375	2.38125	$\frac{11}{32}$	0.34375	8.73125
$\frac{7}{64}$	0.109375	2.778125	$\frac{23}{64}$	0.359375	9.128125
$\frac{1}{8}$	0.125	3.175	$\frac{3}{8}$	0.375	9.525
$\frac{9}{64}$	0.140625	3.571875	$\frac{25}{64}$	0.390625	9.921875
$\frac{5}{32}$	0.15625	3.96875	$\frac{13}{32}$	0.40625	10.31875
$\frac{11}{64}$	0.171875	4.365625	$\frac{27}{64}$	0.421875	10.715625
$\frac{3}{16}$	0.1875	4.7625	$\frac{7}{16}$	0.4375	11.1125
$\frac{13}{64}$	0.203125	5.159375	$\frac{29}{64}$	0.453125	11.509375
$\frac{7}{32}$	0.21875	5.55625	$\frac{15}{32}$	0.46875	11.90625
$\frac{15}{64}$	0.234375	5.953125	$\frac{31}{64}$	0.484375	12.303125
$\frac{1}{4}$	0.25	6.35001	$\frac{1}{2}$	0.50	12.7

Table of Decimal Inches and Metric Equivalents (*cont.*)

Inch	Decimal Inch	Millimeter	Inch	Decimal Inch	Millimeter
$\frac{33}{64}$	0.515625	13.096875	$\frac{49}{64}$	0.765625	19.446875
$\frac{17}{32}$	0.53125	13.49375	$\frac{25}{32}$	0.78125	19.84375
$\frac{35}{64}$	0.546875	13.890625	$\frac{51}{64}$	0.796875	20.240625
$\frac{9}{16}$	0.5625	14.2875	$\frac{13}{16}$	0.8125	20.6375
$\frac{37}{64}$	0.578125	14.684375	$\frac{53}{64}$	0.828125	21.034375
$\frac{19}{32}$	0.59375	15.08125	$\frac{27}{32}$	0.84375	21.43125
$\frac{39}{64}$	0.609375	15.478125	$\frac{55}{64}$	0.859375	21.828125
$\frac{5}{8}$	0.625	15.875	$\frac{7}{8}$	0.875	22.225
$\frac{41}{64}$	0.640625	16.271875	$\frac{57}{64}$	0.890625	22.621875
$\frac{21}{32}$	0.65625	16.66875	$\frac{29}{32}$	0.90625	23.01875
$\frac{43}{64}$	0.671875	17.065625	$\frac{59}{64}$	0.921875	23.415625
$\frac{11}{16}$	0.6875	17.4625	$\frac{15}{16}$	0.9375	23.8125
$\frac{45}{64}$	0.703125	17.859375	$\frac{61}{64}$	0.953125	24.209375
$\frac{23}{32}$	0.71875	18.25625	$\frac{31}{32}$	0.96875	24.60625
$\frac{47}{64}$	0.734375	18.653125	$\frac{63}{64}$	0.984375	25.003125
$\frac{3}{4}$	0.75	19.05	I	1.00000	25.4

Bibliography Works Cited in the Text

ALTENBURG, J. E. *Versuch einer Einleitung zur heroisch-musikalischen Trompeter- und Pauker-Kunst.* Halle: J. C. Hendel, 1795.

BENADE, A. H. *Horns, Strings, and Harmony.* New York: Doubleday, Anchor Books, 1960.

BESSARABOFF, N. *Ancient European Musical Instruments.* Cambridge, Mass.: Harvard University Press, 1941.

BRAND, E. D. *Band Instrument Repairing Manual.* (Copies may be obtained from E. D. Brand, 1117 W. Beardsley Avenue, Elkhart, Indiana 46514.)

BROUGH, J. C. S. *Timbers for Woodwork.* London: Evans Brothers, 1967.

CONSTANTINE, A., Jr. *Know Your Woods.* New York: Albert Constantine and Son, 1969.

DIDEROT, D., ed. *L'Encyclopédie.* Volumes of plates. Paris: Briasson, David, LeBreton and Durand, 1762–72. Facsimile edition. 5 vols. New York: Readex Microprint Corporation, 1969.

EDLIN, H. L. *What Wood is That?* New York: Viking Press, 1969.

EICHBORN, H. *Die Trompete.* Leipzig: Breitkopf and Härtel, 1881.

FINE HARDWOODS ASSOCIATION, *Fine Hardwoods Selectorama.* Chicago.

HALFPENNY, E. "William Bull and the English Baroque Trumpet." *Galpin Society Journal* 15 (1962): 18–24.

———. "Early British Trumpet Mouthpieces." *Galpin Society Journal* 20 (1967): 76–88.

———. "Four Seventeenth Century British Trumpets." *Galpin Society Journal* 22 (1969): 51–57.

MAHILLON, V. C. *Éléments d'Acoustique.* Brussels: C. Mahillon, 1874.

MARVIN, R. "Recorders and English Flutes in European Collections." *Galpin Society Journal* 25 (1972): 30–57.

RENDLE, B. J. *World Timbers.* 3 vols. London: Ernest Benn, 1969.

SMITHERS, D. "The Trumpets of J. W. Haas." *Galpin Society Journal* 18 (1965): 23–41.

TOMLIN, P. "Woodwind Instruments." *Woodworker* 75 (1971): 118, 131, 199, 234, 303, 326, 344.

WHEELER, J. "Further Notes on the British Trumpet." *Galpin Society Journal* 18 (1965): 14–22.

YOUNG, T. C. *The Making of Musical Instruments.* Oxford: Oxford University Press, 1939. Reprint. Freeport, N.Y.: Books for Libraries, 1969.

General Books on the History of Musical Instruments

BAINES, A. *Woodwind Instruments and their History*, 3d ed. New York: W. W. Norton, 1967.

———. *European and American Musical Instruments.* London: Batsford, 1966.

———., ed. *Musical Instruments Through the Ages.* Harmondsworth, Eng.: Penguin Books, 1961.

BATE, P. *The Flute.* New York: W. W. Norton, 1969.

———. *The Oboe*, 2d ed. New York: W. W. Norton, 1962.

———. *The Trumpet and Trombone.* New York: W. W. Norton, 1966.

BRAGARD, R. and DE HEN, F. J. *Musical Instruments in Art and History.* London: Barrie and Rockliff, 1968.

BUCHNER, A. *Musical Instruments Through the Ages.* London: Spring Books, 1961.

CARSE, A. *Musical Wind Instruments*. New York: Da Capo Press, 1965.

GALPIN, F. W. *Old English Instruments of Music*, 3d ed. London: Methuen, 1965.

HARRISON, F. and RIMMER, J. *European Musical Instruments*. New York: W. W. Norton, 1964.

HUNT, E. *The Recorder and Its Music*. New York: W. W. Norton, 1963.

KROLL, O. *The Clarinet*. London: Batsford, 1968.

LANGWILL, L. G. *The Bassoon and Contrabassoon*. New York: W. W. Norton, 1966.

MARCUSE, S. *Musical Instruments, A Comprehensive Dictionary*. New York: Doubleday, 1964.

MELVILLE-MASON, G., ed. *An Exhibition of European Musical Instruments*. London: The Galpin Society, 1968.

MERSENNE, MARIN, *Harmonie Universelle*. 1636. Reprint. Centre National de la Recherche Scientifique, Paris, 1965. English translation by R. E. Chapman, The Hague: Nijhoff, 1957.

RENDALL, F. G. *The Clarinet*, 2d ed. New York: W. W. Norton, 1967.

ROCKSTRO, R. S. *A Treatise on the Flute*. London: Musica Rara, 1967.

SACHS, C. *Real-Lexicon der Musikinstrumente*. 1913. Reprint. New York: Dover Publications, 1964.

WINTERNITZ, E. *Musical Instruments of the Western World*. New York: McGraw Hill, 1966.